THE CIVIL WAR MEMOIRS OF
CAPTAIN WILLIAM J. SEYMOUR

THE CIVIL WAR
MEMOIRS OF
CAPTAIN
WILLIAM J. SEYMOUR

Reminiscences of a Louisiana Tiger

EDITED, WITH AN INTRODUCTION, BY

Terry L. Jones

LOUISIANA STATE UNIVERSITY PRESS

Baton Rouge and London

Copyright © 1991 by Louisiana State University Press
All rights reserved
Manufactured in the United States of America
First printing
00 99 98 97 96 95 94 93 92 91   5 4 3 2 1
Designer: Patricia Douglas Crowder
Typeface: Linotron 202 Bembo
Typesetter: G & S Typesetters, Inc.
Printer and binder: Thomson-Shore, Inc.

LIBRARY OF CONGRESS CATALOGING-IN-PUBLICATION DATA

Seymour, William J.
    The Civil War memoirs of Captain William J. Seymour: reminiscences of a Louisiana
Tiger / edited by Terry L. Jones.
        p.   cm.
    Includes bibliographical references and index.
    ISBN 0-8071-1646-7 (cloth)
    1. Seymour, William J.   2. United States—History—Civil War, 1861–1865—Personal
narratives, Confederate.   3. Louisiana—History—Civil War, 1861–1865—Personal
narratives.   4. Fort Jackson (La.)—Siege, 1862.   5. Soldiers—Louisiana—
Biography.   I. Jones, Terry L., 1952–   . II. Title.
E605.S54   1991
973.7'82—dc20   90-49919
                                                                                                          CIP

Captain William J. Seymour's memoirs are reprinted with the
permission of the William L. Clements Library, University of Michigan,
Ann Arbor.

The paper in this book meets the guidelines for permanence and durability
of the Committee on Production Guidelines for Book Longevity of the
Council on Library Resources. ∞

For Laura and Amie

CONTENTS

MAPS

ACKNOWLEDGMENTS

Editing the Seymour memoirs has been a pleasurable experience, and I have been aided immeasurably by many people. I would like to express my gratitude to John C. Dann, director of the William L. Clements Library, University of Michigan at Ann Arbor, for graciously allowing me the opportunity to edit and publish the Seymour manuscript. To Galen R. Wilson, former manuscript curator of the William L. Clements Library, go my many thanks for his assistance in researching the collection. Doyle Harrison, Ben Schley, and Terry Waxham all provided valuable information during personal interviews, and Gary Joiner did an excellent job on short notice in producing the maps. The archival staffs at Duke University, Durham, North Carolina; the Library of Congress and National Archives, Washington, D.C.; Louisiana State University, Baton Rouge, Louisiana; New York City Public Library, New York City; Northwestern State University, Natchitoches, Louisiana; Southern Historical Collection, University of North Carolina, Chapel Hill; and Tulane University, New Orleans, Louisiana, were, as usual, indispensable in making available their various collections.

To Margaret Dalrymple, John Easterly, and Catherine Landry of the Louisiana State University Press, I would like to express my sincere gratitude for their help and patience with me. Trudie Calvert, my copy editor, did her usual fine job in cleaning up the manuscript for publication, and I thank her.

Finally, to my wife, Carol, I say thanks for being as patient and understanding as usual.

THE CIVIL WAR MEMOIRS OF
CAPTAIN WILLIAM J. SEYMOUR

INTRODUCTION

I N a postwar newspaper article, former Confederate officer William Johnson Seymour revealed that he had kept a private journal during the 1862 Union siege of Fort Jackson, Louisiana.[1] From this obscure beginning emerged an engaging tale of bivouac and battle with Louisiana troops during the Civil War. Sometime between 1865 and 1886 Seymour apparently used his journal as the basis for detailed reminiscences of his years in the service. Being a newspaper editor, Seymour recorded both major events and illuminating details of life in the Confederate army with the eye of a reporter. Seymour's story is particularly rewarding today because it is the only known narrative of length by a Confederate at Fort Jackson (aside from official reports) or by any field or staff officer in the famed 1st Louisiana Brigade of the Army of Northern Virginia. Unfortunately, the present location of Seymour's original war journal is unknown—and it is not even certain when the subsequent memoirs were written.

In 1948, for one hundred dollars, the University of Michigan at Ann Arbor purchased the Seymour Collection from a New York City manuscript dealer. Originally, the two-volume journal had belonged to William's father, Colonel Isaac Gurdon Seymour, of the 6th Louisiana Volunteers. The first volume is stamped in gold "Drill Manual of Col. I. G. Seymour, 6th La. Regt." and has fifty-five pages of the colonel's handwritten drill commands. Then begins a narrative in William's handwriting entitled "Private Journal During the Confederate War, William J. Seymour." This covers Seymour's activities from March, 1862, to October, 1864. A second, smaller volume contains a slightly different version of the same narrative,

1. Ex-Confederate Officer [William J. Seymour], "Annals of the War: The Bombardment of Forts Jackson and St. Philip," newspaper clipping, in Isaac G. Seymour Papers, Schoff Civil War Collection, University of Michigan, Ann Arbor.

along with some handwritten passages from *Macbeth* in Colonel Seymour's handwriting.

Captain William J. Seymour's reminiscences are generally very legible and well written, but at times he had difficulty with spelling, sentence structure, and punctuation. This edited work has kept faithful to his original writing as much as possible. For example, there have been no attempts to correct his misspellings or point them out by inserting [sic]. To do so would disrupt the narrative unnecessarily. But at times Seymour tended to write extremely long, run-on sentences that can be confusing. Therefore, a few punctuation changes have been made, and some of the confusing sentences have been broken down into simpler ones. None of this minor editing has affected the intent or content of the manuscript.

The Seymours were part of the Connecticut Seymour family and were distant relatives of Horatio Seymour, onetime presidential candidate. Isaac G. Seymour was born in October, 1804, in Savannah, Georgia, and graduated with honors from Yale University in 1825. In 1827 he moved to Macon, Georgia, to open a law office and two years later married Caroline E. Whitlock. Tragically, the couple lost three children in infancy and a daughter, Catherine, at age nineteen. Seymour soon found publishing more enjoyable than law and in 1832 became editor of the *Georgia Messenger,* a position he kept for seventeen years. He later was elected to the city council, became known as an active Whig spokesman, and in 1833 began a six-year stint as Macon's first mayor.

Isaac found that he also had a military calling. When war erupted with the Seminole Indians in 1836, he was elected captain of the Macon Volunteers and served in Florida. General Winfield Scott was impressed with Seymour and offered him a commission in the regular army. Seymour was flattered but declined. He could not escape the military, however. When the Mexican War began, Seymour raised a battalion of cavalry and again donned a uniform for his country. Scott, again Seymour's commanding general, made him military governor of Santa Anna's home, the Castle of Perote. When Santa Anna left Mexico for Jamaica, Seymour escorted him to the coast.

At the end of the Mexican War in 1848, Seymour moved his family to New Orleans, where he became editor and partner in the New

Orleans *Commercial Bulletin,* the city's leading financial newspaper.[2] Seymour's only surviving son, William Johnson Seymour, was born May 12, 1832, in Macon but did not initially accompany the family to New Orleans. William enrolled in Hobart College in New York State but apparently did not graduate. He left school and moved to New Orleans to become an assistant editor and partner in the *Commercial Bulletin.* By 1860 the Seymour family was a potent force in New Orleans society.[3]

When war clouds gathered in 1861, Isaac returned to the military. Offering his services to his adopted state, he was soon elected colonel of the largely Irish 6th Louisiana Volunteers. When his regiment was ordered to Virginia, Isaac had no choice but to turn over the reins of the *Commercial Bulletin* to William. This large responsibility concerned Isaac. To a friend he wrote, "William has arrived at that age that he must rely upon himself. He has the whole business given to him and he must depend upon his own wit. . . to carry it through."[4]

William chafed under this responsibility and badly wanted to get into the war. In December, Brigadier General Richard Taylor, son of former president Zachary Taylor and commander of the 1st Louisiana Brigade in Virginia, offered William an appointment as his aide-de-camp. Seymour was forced to decline, however, because of his sense of duty to his father and their newspaper. But by spring of 1862, he could wait no longer and accepted the position of volunteer aide to Brigadier General Johnson Kelly Duncan, his future wife's brother-in-law. Duncan was given command of the coastal defenses of New Orleans, and in late March he and Seymour traveled to Fort Jackson, the main fortification protecting the city, some seventy-five miles downstream. For the next month Seymour was subjected to the brutal and sometimes spectacular realities of war. Surviving a tremendous bombardment by the United States Navy,

2. New Orleans *Commercial Bulletin,* July 30, 1862, in New Orleans Civil War Scrapbook II, Tulane University, New Orleans; Ida Young, Julius Gholson, and Clara Nell Hargrove, *History of Macon, Georgia* (Macon, 1950), 308; Napier Bartlett, *Military Record of Louisiana* (Baton Rouge, 1964), 32–33; Isaac G. Seymour, Yale University Diploma, in Seymour Papers.

3. William J. Seymour obituary, newspaper clipping, November 11, 1886, in Seymour Papers.

4. Isaac G. Seymour to "Sir," September 2, 1861, *ibid.*

he was among those Confederate soldiers who surrendered to federal forces on April 28, 1862.

The Yankees paroled Seymour, and he returned to his newspaper in New Orleans, where he soon ran afoul of the infamous Major General Benjamin "Beast" Butler, commander of the occupying federal troops. In violation of Butler's censorship decree, Seymour published a patriotic obituary of his father after Colonel Seymour was killed in battle at Gaines' Mill, Virginia. Seymour was arrested and, ironically, was incarcerated in Fort Jackson from August 1 to October 17, 1862, at which time he was paroled by Butler.

There followed a brief respite before the war swept him up again. On October 27 he married Elizabeth Berthoud Grimshaw. Little is known of "Lizzy" except that she was the daughter of an Englishman who worked as a merchant in New Orleans, was of dark complexion with dark hair and gray eyes, stood five feet, five inches tall, and was twenty-three or twenty-four years old.[5] Soon after the wedding, Seymour moved his new bride out of occupied New Orleans to safety in his old hometown of Macon, Georgia.

By the spring of 1863, Seymour had won a new position as volunteer aide to Brigadier General Harry T. Hays, who replaced Richard Taylor as commander of the 1st Louisiana Brigade, Army of Northern Virginia. For the next year and a half, he served with some of the South's most famous officers and fought with the army through the major campaigns from Chancellorsville to Cedar Creek. During this time, Seymour was promoted to captain and was appointed brigade assistant adjutant general. From his position as staff officer, Seymour saw the Confederate command system up close and formed strong opinions on how campaigns and battles were conducted. He was also a meticulous observer of details and kept a private journal. When he subsequently wrote his war memoirs, Seymour gave free rein to his opinions, and his journal observations allowed him to recreate long-past incidents with great clarity. The narrative begins with Fort Jackson.

5. Seymour obituary, November 15, 1886, newspaper clipping; Seymour marriage license; Seymour loyalty oath, May 5, 1865, all *ibid.*

FORT JACKSON

WHEN the Civil War began in April, 1861, the South realized that its largest and most important city—New Orleans— would be an early target of the federal forces. The city's defenses were entrusted to Brigadier General Johnson Kelly Duncan, a thirty-five-year-old Pennsylvania native and 1849 graduate of West Point. He had resigned his commission in 1855 to become superintendent of government construction in New Orleans. Duncan was chief engineer of the Louisiana Board of Public Works when war broke out and reentered the military to become brigadier general in command of the New Orleans coastal defenses.[1] Protection of the city depended almost solely on Forts Jackson and St. Philip, some seventy-five miles to the south. Located seven hundred yards apart on opposite banks of the Mississippi River, these forts were part of the permanent defenses of the United States and were seized by the Louisiana militia on January 10, 1861. They were a short distance above a sharp bend in the river, and river traffic had to reduce speed to negotiate the curve and swift current. In days past, the forts had seemed impregnable, but in 1861 they were badly deteriorated and needed modern guns.[2]

Of the two, Fort Jackson, named for Andrew Jackson, was by far the more important. Its construction had begun in 1822. Set on the west bank, this pentagon-shaped bastion boasted a 110-yard front and 22-foot-high brick walls. Its casemated guns were largely bombproof and were supported by a water battery. A deep ditch ringed the fortress, and clear fields of fire had been created by felling intervening trees. The armament of Fort Jackson consisted of approximately seventy-five guns, ranging from six-

1. Ezra J. Warner, *Generals in Gray: Lives of the Confederate Commanders* (Baton Rouge, 1959), 77–78; New Orleans *Times-Picayune*, December 26, 1915.
2. John D. Winters, *The Civil War in Louisiana* (Baton Rouge, 1963), 10, 18, 65–66; Fletcher Pratt, *Civil War on Western Waters* (New York, 1956), 33; Powell A. Casey, *Encyclopedia of Forts, Posts, Named Camps, and Other Military Installations in Louisiana, 1700–1981* (Baton Rouge, 1983), 79.

pound smoothbores to ten-inch Columbiads. There were, however, precious few of the large guns and rifled weapons that were desperately needed to stop any modern river fleet. The fort was further weakened by its garrison of foreign-born and former northerners. Most of these men had to be forced to leave New Orleans for the forts, and some of the militia mutinied and had to be prodded aboard the ships with bayonets. Nearly all of these disgruntled soldiers hoped the Yankees would not attempt a passage of the forts.[3]

To impede any attempt to run by the forts, a boom made of huge cypress logs chained together was strung across the river and anchored both to the river bottom and to each bank. Above this barricade was assembled a motley assortment of water craft intended to engage the Union fleet. This ragtag navy consisted of Confederate and state naval gunboats, converted tugs, and other odd vessels—approximately a dozen in all, bearing forty-two guns. Some forty to fifty fire rafts loaded with pine logs soaked in turpentine and tar filled out the mongrel fleet.[4]

By the end of March, 1862, the Union fleet had entered the Mississippi River and anchored at Pilot Town. Commanded by Captain David Farragut, the fleet consisted of seventeen men-of-war, twenty mortar boats, and seven gunboats and carried an impressive 268 guns. Farragut's mortar boats were under the command of Commodore David Porter, the son of Farragut's adopted father. Farragut and Porter were confident that the passage of the forts would be easy. Porter even boasted that the thirteen-inch shells of his mortar boats would batter down the forts within forty-eight hours. The contest began in early April.[5]

I N December 1861, Brig. Genl. Richard Taylor, Commanding [the] First Louisiana Brigade, [Thomas J. "Stonewall"] Jackson's Corps, Army of Northern Virginia, tendered me the appointment of aide-de-camp on his Staff. My Father, who commanded the Sixth Louisiana Regt. of that Brigade, informed me by letter that if I accepted this appointment he would be

---

3. Winters, *Civil War in Louisiana,* 84, 86; Pratt, *Civil War on Western Waters,* 33.
4. *Official Records of the Union and Confederate Navies in the War of the Rebellion* (30 vols.; Washington, D.C., 1894–1922), Ser. I, Vol. XVIII, 323–24 (hereinafter cited as *ORN*); Winters, *Civil War in Louisiana,* 66, 89; Pratt, *Civil War on Western Waters,* 35, 44–45.
5. *ORN,* XVIII, 361; Pratt, *Civil War on Western Waters,* 72–75.

compelled, greatly against his will, to throw up his commission and return to New Orleans to take charge of the "Commercial Bulletin" newspaper, then being conducted by me. Knowing that such a course would be exceedingly distasteful to him, he being passionately fond of military life, I reluctantly declined the proffered appointment.

On the 13th of March, 1862, I was appointed Volunteer Aide-de-Camp to Brig. Genl. J[ohnson] K. Duncan, Commanding the Coast Defenses of Louisiana. Upon the receipt of information that a large fleet of Federal vessels were crossing the bars of the Mississippi River for the purpose of attacking the Forts, situated seventy-nine miles below New Orleans, I accompanied General Duncan to Fort Jackson on the 28th of March, 1862. This Fort is on the right bank of the River, and almost directly opposite is Fort St. Philip; upon these two forts the Confederate authorities depended for the defence of the River approach to the City. In the two works there were about one hundred and ten guns mounted, but they were for the most part of too small calibre for "guns of position," being 32 & 24 pounders, with eight inch Columbiads[6]—altogether too light to cope successfully with the 9 & 11 inch Dalghrens[7] & the 13 inch mortars which formed the armament of the Federal fleet. Gen. Duncan had fully represented this fact to the Secretary of War, Mr. [Judah P.] Benjamin,[8] and repeatedly and strongly urged upon him the necessity of furnishing the Forts with larger guns. But that functionary, who was miserably deficient in those qualifications that are requisite in an efficient War Secretary, turned a deaf ear to the General's importunities and very confidently asserted that the Forts, in the condition they were then in, could stop any fleet that might attempt to ascend the River. Great stress was laid on the fact

6. Columbiads were huge smoothbore cannons that fired large shells at a high angle of elevation. They were popular for defending channels and coastlines. See Patricia L. Faust, ed., *Historical Times Illustrated Encyclopedia of the Civil War* (New York, 1986), 153.

7. Dahlgrens were smoothbore guns, invented by Admiral John A. Dahlgren, designed for use against wooden ships. They were also found to be useful against ironclads. *Ibid.*, 202.

8. Judah P. Benjamin was a prominent New Orleans attorney and politician who strongly supported secession. Jefferson Davis appointed him as the first attorney general of the Confederacy in February, 1861, and secretary of war in September, 1861. Although he was very close to Davis, his haughty attitude caused many to dislike him. During the short life of the Confederacy he also held the position of secretary of state. *Ibid.*, 54–55.

Forts Jackson and St. Philip

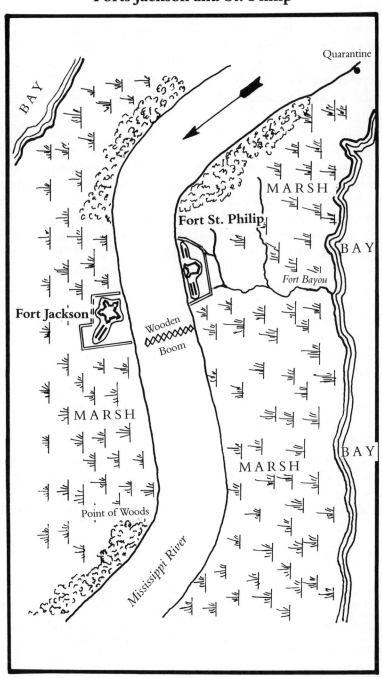

BAY

Quarantine

MARSH

Fort St. Philip

BAY

Fort Bayou

Fort Jackson

Wooden
Boom

MARSH

BAY

Point of Woods

MARSH

BAY

Mississippi River

that in 1815, Fort St. Philip alone was able to successfully resist the passage of the River by the English Squadron; but the astute Secretary did not bear in mind that the British had no others but sailing vessels, while the Federals' fleet consisted of twenty-seven swift-running & powerfully armed steamers, besides mortar vessels.[9]

Despairing of obtaining timely assistance from the General Government, the Confederate authorities in Louisiana, the Governor of the State, & the Citizens of New Orleans went to work to prepare as best they could for the defense of the City. Money was lavishly subscribed; eighty ten inch Columbiads were ordered to be cast at the different Foundries in the city; a number of tow boats and Steam-ships were converted into war steamers, protected by cotton bulk-heads; and the construction of two iron clads was commenced. But, unfortunately, we had relied too much & too long upon getting assistance from the Government, and the above preparations could not be consummated before the attack was commenced. The heavy guns were never finished; the cotton-clad boats, of which great expectation had been formed, proved to be no match for the enemy's war-steame[r]s, and were all, with one or two exceptions, knocked to pieces or set on fire in a very few minutes at the passage of the Forts. Of the two iron clads, one [*Mississippi*] was never so far completed as to be armed, while the other [*Louisiana*] was carried to the Forts when she could only be used during the bombardment as a floating battery, and that not effectively.

In the month of February a raft was built across the River some three hundred yards below Fort Jackson, under the direction of Major [R.] Montague;[10] it was constructed of logs strongly chained together in sections, each section held in its place by an anchor. Under ordinary circumstances this obstruction would, no doubt, have answered the purpose for which it was built, viz. to prevent

9. Secretary of War Benjamin's view that the forts' existing armament could stop the Union fleet was widely held in New Orleans. In 1815 Fort St. Philip withstood a ten-day bombardment from the English fleet and suffered only two fatalities. But in 1862 steam-powered ships could run past the forts quickly, and such military innovations as flat-shooting rifled cannons could batter down the forts more easily. Samuel Carter III, *Blaze of Glory: The Fight for New Orleans, 1814–1815* (New York, 1971), 286–88.

10. Major R. Montague was a member of the 1st Louisiana Heavy Artillery. Compiled Service Records of Confederate General and Staff Officers, and Nonregimental Enlisted Men, War Record Group 109, Microcopy 331, Roll 180, National Archives.

the enemy's vessels from moving past the Forts. But it unfortunately happened that the River during this season rose to an unwanted heighth; the current was thereby greatly accelerated and vast quantities of drift wood were floated down against the raft, which, though every effort was made to relieve it as much as possible of this immense pressure, was swept from it's moorings & carried through the Passes far out to sea. Lt. Col. [Edward] Higgins[11] afterwards attempted to place an obstruction at the same point; this consisted of a line of schooners, anchored at short intervals with bows up stream, and thoroughly chained together amid ships as well as by stem & stern. The running rigging, rattlings & cables were left to trail astern of these schooners as an additional impediment to tangle in the propeller wheels of the enemy's vessels. This obstruction also proved ineffectual, as will be seen hereafter.

Pensacola [Florida], having been evacuated by the Confederate Army under Genl. [Braxton] Bragg,[12] Gen. Duncan dispatched his brother, Major W[illia]m P. Duncan, to that place to take possession of any pieces of heavy ordnance that might be found remaining there unappropriated. Major Duncan found and sent to the Forts the following guns: three 10 inch Columbiads; three 8 inch Columbiads, one 42 pounder rifled gun, and five 10 inch sea-coast mortars.[13] These, with a seven inch rifle gun (of the Brooke patent),[14] were the only additions made to the armament of the Forts.

When the General & I arrived at Fort Jackson, we found the garrison in a very uncomfortable situation. The extraordinarily high stage of water in the River and the continued prevalence of Easterly gales had caused the water to rise in the Fort, and a considerable portion of the parade plaine and the floors of a number of the case-

11. Higgins, a Confederate army regular officer, was in command of Fort Jackson. Ex-officer, "Bombardment of Forts Jackson and St. Philip," in Seymour Papers.

12. General Braxton Bragg, an adopted son of Louisiana, was ordered to take control of Pensacola in early 1861. He evacuated the city a year later after the fall of Forts Henry and Donelson to reinforce Tennessee. Faust, *Encyclopedia of the Civil War,* 75, 574.

13. Official records credit Major Duncan with securing only three 10-inch Columbiads and five mortars. *ORN,* XVIII, 254.

14. The Brooke rifle was invented by the chief of the Confederate navy's Bureau of Ordnance, John Mercer Brooke. To allow for higher pressures, the cast-iron gun had wrought-iron reinforcing bands around the breech and barrel. It was considered one of the war's finest artillery pieces. Faust, *Encyclopedia of the Civil War,* 81.

mates were submerged to a depth of from 10 to 15 inches. A trench was cut around the main magazine & it required constant pumping to prevent our ammunition from being spoilt. The garrison was put to work at mounting the heavy guns that had been brought over from Pensacola, which was very severe labor owing to the high water and the soft, yielding condition of the ground over which the guns and carriages had to be transported. Sand bags were placed over the two magazines to protect them from the effects of a vertical (mortar) fire and the old water battery back of Fort Jackson, which had never been armed and the traces of which had become almost obliterated by the action of many storms and the rank growth of weeds, was put in order and guns mounted thereon. To accomplish all this the men soon worked by reliefs, day and night; and on the 13th of April every thing had been done, with the limited amount of material at hand, which human energy and skill could accomplish to prepare the Fort for the coming conflict.

A large number of rafts loaded with light wood had been brought down from the city & moored above the Forts for the purpose of being ignited & turned loose to drift down the River among the enemy's ships. The following steamers, protected by cotton bulkheads and prepared with iron prows to act as rams, were sent down to assist in the defense of the Forts. The *Warrior, Stonewall Jackson, Defiance* and *Resolute, Governor Moore,* and *General Quitman*—commanded respectively by Captain [John A.] Stephenson [Stevenson], [George M.] Phil[l]ips, [Joseph D.] McCoy, [Isaac] Hooper, Beverly Kennon & Alex[ander] Grant. Subsequently, the C. S. Steamers *Manassas* (iron clad ram), Capt. [Alexander F.] Warley; *Jackson,* Capt. [Francis B.] Renshaw & *McRae,* Capt. [Thomas B.] Huger, arrived.

A Regiment of infantry under command of Col. [Ignatius] Sysmoinsks [Szymanski] was stationed at the Quarantine Station—seven miles above the Forts—to establish picket posts at the heads of the canals leading from the River into the bays back of the Station, to guard against a land force being thrown above us by means of launches. A company of sharpshooters, under command of Capt. W. G. Mullen, was placed in the woods on the right bank of the River, 2½ miles below Fort Jackson to pick off the officers on board the enemy's vessels when they should come up on reconnoiting expeditions.[15] The above comprise the preparation made to resist the passage of the enemy's fleet up the River.

On the 10th & 11th of April the raft of schooners was badly damaged by the high winds that then prevailed, which damage was greatly increased by several "fire rafts" breaking loose from their moorings & drifting against it, parting the chain cables & scattering most of the schooners. This we regarded as a great calamity, for we had depended upon this raft to detain the enemy's ships under our fire long enough for us to seriously damage them, if not to destroy most of them. The sharpshooters, most of whom were stationed at the Point of Woods,[16] accomplished little or nothing, owing to the high water, and after remaining there three days, they were withdrawn and sent back to town. The fire rafts upon which we relied to disturb the enemy's fleet after it had taken a position and to keep the river well lighted up so that we could frustrate any attempt that might be made by the Yankee steamers to dash past the Forts under cover of darkness, proved to be, for the most part, failures, owing to the lack of skill & judgment displayed by the officers of the River Fleet who had them in charge.

We had a line of telegraph wire extending to within half of a mile of "The Jump,"[17] nine miles below Fort Jackson & a steamer was sent down the River every day as near as possible to the Heads of the Passes for the purpose of reconnoiting the enemy; while scouts, skiffs & pirougues, were operating in the bays to the East & West of the River, to keep us advised of the enemy's movements.

The enemy kept 10 to 12 of his light draft Steamers at the Heads of the Passes, 22 miles below Fort Jackson for the purpose of concealing this movement, while he was working his larger ships over the South West Bar, he having failed to effect an entrance by way of Pass a l'Outre.[18]

---

15. Mullen commanded approximately two hundred sharpshooters. They were mostly "swamp hunters" and riffraff from New Orleans and were not at all happy with their assignment. *ORN*, XVIII, 254, 391.

16. The Point of Woods was the broad point of land created on the inward curve of the river below the fort. It was a low, swampy peninsula covered with live oak trees.

17. The Jump was a pass running through the west bank of the river into West Bay. *ORN*, XVIII, 362.

18. Farragut's fleet actually crossed over the South West Bar in late March and assembled

April 9th. On this day while our working parties were busily engaged in mounting guns and strengthening our defenses, a brisk
cannonading was heard from the direction of the Hds. of the Passes.
The long roll was beaten & officers & men went quickly to quarters.
The firing sounding nearer and nearer, we knew that the Yankees
were in chase of our reconnoitring Steamer, a large, unarmed tow
boat called the *Star*.[19] So we loaded several of the heaviest guns in
the Fort and stood ready to protect the *Star* and give the enemy's
boats a warm reception when they should come within range. In a
short time the *Star* made her appearance, steaming very rapidly
around the "Point of Woods," closely pursued by two gunboats,
which fired their bow chasers as rapidly as they could be loaded.
The chase was a very exciting one, the enemy's shells bursting
thickly above and around the old *Star* and we momentarily expected to see her struck and disabled, for being a high pressure boat
her machinery was all on deck & unprotected. But the noble craft
kept on her course and soon found a safe refuge under the guns of
the Forts. The two pursuing gunboats had the temerity to come
within range of our heaviest guns, when we quickly opened upon
them. The firing on our side was excellent; the second shell from
one of our 10 inch Columbiads passing between the masts of one of
the Yankee vessels. The enemy were in a few moments brought to a
realizing sense of the perils of his situation, and the two saucy vessels dropped down behind the Point and out of range of our guns.
Soon afterwards they steamed rapidly down the River and rejoined
the fleet at the Head of the Passes. This was the enemy's first
reconnoissance.

Nothing of interest occurred until the 13th. In the meantime the
garrison was busily engaged in strenthing the Forts as much as
possible.

April 13th. During this day the Federal gunboats came within
sight to make observations. They would occasionally show themselves singly or in pairs. Keeping themselves close to the opposite

---

at Pilot Town. The fleet consisted of seventeen men-of-war, Porter's twenty mortar boats,
and seven gunboats. *Ibid.,* 361; Winters, *Civil War in Louisiana,* 85.

19. The *Star* was a 250-ton unarmed steamer that was used as a telegraph station below
the fort. Apparently the *Star* tapped into telegraph wire that was strung to Pilot Town. *ORN,*
XVIII, 250, 683.

shore they would throw a few shells at the Fort, to which we would respond, when they would retire behind the Point. Our sharpshooters annoyed them, owing to the high water in the swamp preventing them from obtaining good positions—the men being, in most cases, up to their waists in water. The blue-coated gentry of "Uncle Sam's" ships were considerably exasperated by the whistling of "Rebel" minies about their heads, so they hauld off to a safe distance and spitefully shelled the woods that contained the bloodthirsty sharpshooters—making a great noise, but doing no other damage than to tear and mutilate the branches and trunks of the gigantic live-oaks that there aboundist.

April 14th. Finding that our sharpshooters would greatly annoy him while placing his ships and mortar vessels in position, the enemy determined to dislodge them; so he brought up several of his gunboats and passed most of the day in pouring a furious storm of grape, cannister & spherical case into the woods to dislodge them. This he finally succeeded in doing and the sharpshooters were brought up to the Fort and there being no other place on the River where they could operate effectively, they were sent up to the city, to the apparent great joy and relief of most, if not all of them. These men were amateur rifle shots from New Orleans who came down to the Forts with very exalted ideas of their skill & prowess; they were unused to privations and hardships, and their four days sojourn in the swamp had made many of them sick, and all of them disgusted with that kind of service. When they returned they were in a most pitiable plight; many of them had lost their shoes in the tenacious mud—their cloths were torn and soiled and their warlike ardor seemed to be considerably cooled by their experiences "by flood & field."

The Federals landed at our Telegraph Station, nine miles below the fort, destroyed the poles & cut the wires. The operator made a narrow escape with his instrument. Efforts were made to re-establish telegraphic communication, also to place sharpshooters further down the River, but they were unsuccessful, owing to the excessive high water.

April 15th. The excitement increases as the movements of the enemy show that the day of trial and conflict draws near. The hostile ships all came out of the Passes into the River and extended from the Point of Woods to the Heads of the Passes; the tall masts and upperyards of the heavy sloops of war being plainly visible to us above the trees. Now was the favorable time for the fire rafts to do execution, and orders were repeatedly sent by Gen. Duncan to the Commander of our River Fleet [Commander John K. Mitchell] to send them down; but every attempt to do so proved abortive, owing to their being set adrift too soon, and, in consequence, drifting against the banks near the Forts. Chagrined at these failures, the General turned the control of the rafts over to the senior C[onfederate] S[tates] Naval officer, Capt. Renshaw; but he also managed them in a clumsy, bungling & unsatisfactory manner.[20]

April 16th. At half past 7 o'clock in the morning three of the enemy's steam vessels boldly ventured from behind the Point of Woods and opened upon Fort Jackson; three of our guns responded and, though the distance was great (2½ miles), they soon made it too warm for the Yankees to remain there and they retired out of sight. Several times during the day this maneuver was repeated, the enemy evidently trying to ascertain the range of our guns. At 4½ o'clock P.M., the gunboat was run out, which engaged the fort briskly, under cover of which two of their mortar boats were brought out into the stream within plain sight of us, but barely within range of our largest guns. These boats opened fire upon Fort Jackson and continued it for one hour & a half, when some of our shots, falling in dangerous proximity to them, they rejoined the fleet. In this little encounter the inferior quality of our ammunition was very apparent, our powder not being strong enough to prevent our shot and shells from falling short of the proper range of the guns. During the day the Yankee Commodore, Porter, was busily engaged in locating the position of his mortar flotilla, which was composed of twenty-one long, low schooners, each mounting one 13 inch mortar.[21] They were placed close against the bank of the River (on the

20. Although Commander John K. Mitchell was in command of the Confederate naval vessels and, presumably, the fire rafts, Duncan reported ordering Captain John A. Stevenson to send them nightly against the Yankees. But the rafts simply washed ashore and set fire to the fort's warehouses. Disgusted, the general then gave control of the rafts to Captain Renshaw. *Ibid.,* 291; Winters, *Civil War in Louisiana,* 89.

21. There were actually only twenty mortar boats. *ORN,* XVIII, 361.

Fort Jackson side) behind the woods, and their masts were covered with leaves and boughs to prevent our discovering their location. Most of them were out of range of our heaviest guns.

April 17th. Early in the morning of this day, before daylight, a fire raft was successfully sent down the River. It drifted right among the Yankee Fleet and produced a great commotion; shots were fired into the burning mass and it was with the greatest difficulty that they prevented their mortar vessels from catching fire.[22] The result of this experiment showed that these rafts, if they had been properly handled during the bombardment, would have proved exceedingly annoying, if not destructive, to the enemy.

In the afternoon five of our steamers went below the raft—passing through the interval caused by the drifting away of some of the schooners—and exchanged a few shots with the enemy's gunboats, but without any visible effect. Many of us thought that this was very imprudent & injudicious in our naval officers, for it enabled the Yankees to discover the breach that had been made in our schooner-raft.

Attempts were made during the night to send down fire-rafts, but they proved unsuccessful. The movements of the enemy betokened the commencement of the bombardment on the following day and everything was put in readiness for the coming conflict.

Hitherto I had been messing with Drs. [Somerville] Burke & [J. A.] Bradbury, & Lieut. W[illia]m M. Bridges[23] in very comfortable quarters in the Hospital outside of the Fort; but we now moved into the Fort, where our quarters were much more contracted and far less comfortable & pleasant.

April 18th. (Good Friday) At 8½ o'clock a.m.[24] the distant booming of a heavy gun told us that the long expected bombardment had commenced. The first mortar shell fell within the Fort—a striking

22. This raft caused a flurry of activity in Farragut's fleet, when four ships were forced to get under way to meet the threat. After several shots failed to sink it, small boats were dispatched from the warships to tow the flaming raft into midstream; where it would drift harmlessly past the fleet. *Ibid.,* 692.

23. Dr. Burke was the fort's assistant surgeon, Dr. Bradbury was surgeon for the 1st Division of Louisiana Militia, and Captain Bridges served as Duncan's aide-de-camp. *Ibid.,* 275; Andrew B. Booth, comp., *Records of Louisiana Confederate Soldiers and Louisiana Confederate Commands* (3 vols.; New Orleans, 1920), II, 80.

24. Duncan placed the beginning of the bombardment at 6:00 A.M. in one report and 9:00 A.M. in another. *ORN,* XVIII, 266.

proof of the skill of the Yankee gunners and of the accuracy of the calculations of their Engineers. Shell succeeded shell in quick succession, falling within the Fort with almost unvariable certainty.[25] When these ponderous missiles fell on the ramparts or parade plein they sunk into the earth to a distant of six or eight feet, and exploding would tear a hole in the earth large enough to admit a barrel. When they struck the brickwork of the Fort, the crashing noise produced was almost stunning, and the bricks and mortar would fly in all directions. I saw a poor fellow, who had narrowly escaped from being crushed by a falling shell, running away from the place laughing in great glee; but before he had run ten yards the shell exploded, throwing fragments of brick in all directions—one of which struck this man in the back, killing him instantly. This occurred about 10 o'clock a.m. and was the first casualty in the Fort.

At 11 o'clock a.m. the officers' quarters in the two rear bastions were fired & consumed by the enemy's shells, the officers losing their baggage and bedding. During the whole day, the enemy's fire was most rapid and furious, he directing his attention solely to Fort Jackson, it being the nearer & more vulnerable of the two. In addition to the vertical fire from twenty-one 13 inch mortars, we were subjected to the horizontal firing from the long-range rifle[d] guns of the gun boats. Sixteen of the mortar vessels were moored along side of the River bank, behind the woods and not within sight of us; the remaining six hauled out into the stream at an angle with them and just at the extreme range of our heaviest guns.[26] We returned their fire with vigor, though most of our shots fell short owing to the miserable quality of our powder; one of the mortar vessels and one gun boat were disabled, and the others retired behind the woods.[27] During the subsequent bombardment we never caught sight of a mortar vessel, though we heard from them with most disagreeable frequency.

25. The gunboats were stationed 2,830 to 4,500 yards from the fort, each boat firing once every ten minutes. *Ibid.*, 362–64.

26. Seymour was mistaken about the number of mortar boats. There were twenty, fourteen being anchored near the west bank behind the Point of Woods and six near the east bank. *ORN*, XVIII, 265–66.

27. Porter sent five gunboats closer to the fort to draw its fire away from his mortar boats. But he reported that the fort's shelling was so vigorous by mid-day he had to withdraw them out of range. Two boats were damaged and one Union sailor was killed. *Ibid.*, 363–64; Winters, *Civil War in Louisiana*, 87.

The citadel was sadly battered and mutilated. It was set on fire and extinguished several times during the day, but at dusk the flames resisted our utmost efforts to subdue them and [t]his portion of the fort was entirely consumed. The heat of the fire was so intense that the magazine and the shell rooms were in great danger. The whole garrisons were turned out, blankets (wet) were placed over the interior walls of the Fort; a fire engine which had been brought from the city played upon them & by great exertion the fire was confined to the Citadel. Fortunately, when this danger threatened us, and when all the men were exposed, the fire of the enemy ceased—not, as we subsequently found out, from dictates of humanity, but for the purpose of giving some rest to their gunners. By actual count the number of mortar shells thrown at Fort Jackson during this day was 2,997, most of which fell within the Fort, producing much damage and disabling several of our best guns.[28] The casualties were unexpectedly few in number—several men being slightly wounded— owing to the fact that all the men who were not on duty at the the [sic] few heavy guns that were being used, were kept under cover in the casemates. Gen. Duncan used every effort to impress upon the mind of the naval officer having in charge the fire barges the great necessity of sending them down during the night for the purpose of dispersing the mortar flottilla; accordingly several attempts were made to send them down, but, owing to the stupidity of those handling them, they were turned adrift above the raft and floated harmlessly ashore near the Forts.[29]

April 19th. At 6½ o'clock a.m. the huge mortars of Porter's flotilla commenced their hoarse barking at us, raining down during the day a constant storm of great shells, each weighing 225 pounds. Ever and anon an adventurous gunboat would show himself and let fly a shell or two at the Fort, but she could not stand the racket of our Columbiads for more than a few minutes and would retreat behind the woods. One of these saucy craft was badly crippled by our fire

28. Porter claimed that over 1,400 shells were fired at Fort Jackson, with many of those being air bursts because of faulty fuses. But the damage was great and the terre-plein, parade plein, parapets, and casemates were badly shot up, the officers' quarters destroyed, and the citadel consumed by flames. Even more serious was that seven of the fort's cannons had been disabled. *ORN*, XVIII, 265–66, 363–64.

29. When Captain Renshaw released the rafts, he was unaware how close they were to the bank. Caught in an eddy, the rafts floated harmlessly downstream until they burned themselves out. Renshaw saw fit to apologize for the error. *Ibid.*, 323.

and had to be tówed to a place of safety.[30] The enemy's firing was terribly accurate and it was sad to see the damage done to the old Fort; the terre plein, parade plein, parapets and platforms being badly cut up. The walls of the Fort—built more than thirty years ago—were not constructed to resist the impact of shot larger than 42 pounders; consequently, several of the enemy's shells, falling from a very high elevation, penetrated into the casemates. One shell pierced the wall and fell into a shell room filled with fixed amunition; if it had exploded it would have tumbled the whole Fort about our ears and caused great destruction of life, bringing the siege to a premature conclusion. Commodore Porter, having before him a plan of our fortifications obtained from the Government archives at Washington, knew the exact position of our magazines and bestowed upon them much of his attention. The wall over one of the magazines was seriously cracked, notwithstanding the thick covering of sand bags that had been placed over it, and the and the [sic] danger of an explosion of our ammunition seemed imminent. By this day's bombardment, one 10 inch & one 8 inch Columbiad, one 32 & one 24 pounder, and one 10 inch seige mortar [were] disabled in the main work; also, two rifled 32 Pounders in the Water Battery. The *feu infernal* of the enemy's mortars was kept up furiously and continuously during the night.[31]

April 20th. Notwithstanding the rain and very high wind, the bombardment was constant during the day, with an occasional shot from the gunboats.

Between 11 and 12 o'clock at night, one gunboat stole quietly up the River under cover of the intense darkness and attempted to drag off the few schooners remaining in the River near the Fort. It succeeded in disingaging one of them, when guns of the Fort opened

30. During the morning several gunboats moved in close to the fort to fire flat trajectory shells but were driven back by accurate Confederate counterfire. Several Union boats were hit on April 19, including the *Maria J. Carlton,* which was sunk at 9:00 A.M. without loss of life. The *Arletta* was damaged by a shell that killed one man, and the *Oneida* was hit twice, wounding approximately fifteen men. *Ibid.,* 365; Winters, *Civil War in Louisiana,* 88; Ex-officer, "Bombardment of Forts Jackson and St. Philip," in Seymour Papers.

31. It was clear by now that Porter's boast that he would reduce Fort Jackson within forty-eight hours was a hollow one. To maintain pressure on the beleaguered garrison, he ordered each of his mortar boats to fire continuously one shell every thirty minutes. Porter's spirits were lifted later that night when a Confederate deserter was brought in giving a vivid description of the havoc being wrought inside the fort by the mortar fire. Pratt, *Civil War on Western Waters,* 84; Winters, *Civil War in Louisiana,* 88.

upon it, driving it back to the fleet in hot haste.[32] While this was going on, the bombardment was unusually heavy; the enemy using time fuses and bursting their shells above the Fort, the fragments falling in every direction. This was done to drive our men away from the barbette guns, but the noble fellows stood at their posts with unswerving fidelity and bravery. The positive success of this bold excursion on the part of the enemy was ascribable to the neglect of Capt. Renshaw to send fire rafts down to keep the River light up, though Gen. Duncan had repeatedly & urgently requested him to send them down at frequent intervals during the night. I will here state, in justification of Gen. Duncan, that the control & direction of these fire barges had been taken out of his hands by order of Maj. Gen. [Mansfield] Lovell and placed in those of the Senior Naval Officer on board of the River Fleet.[33] During the whole night the mortars firing was kept up with unabated rapidity and fury.

April 21st. Firing continued all day and night.[34] Five of our guns were disabled and several men wounded; the guns were repaired as far as practicable, though our fatigue parties were greatly exposed in so doing. By this time Fort Jackson presented a very dilapidated appearance; many of the casemates were crushed in, a number of the guns had been rendered unserviceable, many large cracks had been made in the main walls, and the sand-bag traverses needed extensive and immediate repairs. Such being the condition of affairs, we were greatly rejoiced to hear of the arrival during the night of the iron-

32. April 20 was Easter Sunday, and Farragut decided to try to break the chain barrier across the river so he could run past the forts at a later date. The *Itasca* and *Pinola* reached the chain and tried to blast it open with a keg of powder, but the detonator failed. The ships finally did manage to break the chain near the east bank and the *Itasca* ran through. Then, while maneuvering to avoid a fire raft, she drifted into the chain and tore a huge hole through it. Although battered, the two vessels made it back to Farragut under Porter's protective fire. Pratt, *Civil War on Western Waters,* 85–86; Winters, *Civil War in Louisiana,* 88.

33. The handling of the fire rafts was a constant source of irritation between Duncan and the Confederate navy. Apparently Major General Mansfield Lovell, who was in overall command of the New Orleans area, insisted that the navy manage the rafts. Because of this and a poor working relationship between the Confederate army and navy, the fire rafts were never deployed in an effective manner. But Seymour is mistaken in claiming no rafts were sent out that night. Several fire rafts were set loose, but only one swept through the chain barrier. It startled the Union fleet, causing two ships to collide in the confusion and suffer serious damage. *ORN,* XVIII, 265–66; Pratt, *Civil War on Western Waters,* 85–86; Warner, *Generals in Gray,* 194–95.

34. By now Porter had divided his mortar boat crews into three shifts of four hours each to give his men time to rest. They were firing approximately 1,500 rounds per day into the fort. *ORN,* XVIII, 366.

clad Steamer *Louisiana,* under cover of whose powerful batteries we expected to make the needed repairs to the Fort. She was encased in iron armor of three inches in thickness—had sloping sides with two wheels amidships and concealed from view, and her armament consisted of sixteen guns of heavy calibre, some of them being 7 inch rifle guns of the Brooke patent—altogether a formidable war vessel.[35]

April 22d. No cessation, or even slacking, of the enemy's fire and their ponderous shells were hurled into the Fort with fatal precision. The Yankees used the Alger fuse[36] in their shells, water tight and made of brass, and very rarely did a shell fail to explode. Those that fell into the water of the moat were unaffected by the water [and] would bury themselves far down into the soft, muddy bottom and explode so violently as to shake the very foundations of the Fort.

Capt. J[ohn] K. Mitchell, Comdg. the *Louisiana,* assumed the command of everything afloat in the River.[37] Gen. Duncan had an interview with him and was much disappointed to learn that the motive power of the *Louisiana* was incomplete, and that there was no probability of her being ready to move by her own propelling power for several days. This information was a serious blow to our hopes of relief from that quarter. The fact being established that the *Louisiana* could not, within a reasonable time, be used for aggressive purposes, Gen. Duncan urged Capt. Mitchell to place her just below the raft, on the Fort St. Philip side of the River and immediately under the guns of both Forts, in which position she could rake and disperse the Mortar Fleet and give us an opportunity to make the necessary repairs to Fort Jackson. The General most earnestly urged this upon Capt. M[itchell], assuring him that if such

35. The *Louisiana* was a formidable ironclad ram that was hastily constructed in New Orleans to meet the Union threat. It was heavily armed with an assortment of smoothbore and rifled guns, but its engines, rudder, and propeller were unfinished when Farragut's fleet arrived. Nonetheless, the garrison of both forts enthusiastically cheered the *Louisiana* when it was towed to a point just above Fort St. Philip on the night of April 21. *Ibid.,* 288; Pratt, *Civil War on Western Waters,* 38–39, 82, 86.

36. The Alger fuse was named for its inventor, Cyrus Alger, and was the most commonly used fuse in the U.S. Navy. The fuse was waterproof by virtue of a crooked powder channel that kept out water. Interview with Terry Waxham, October 23, 1987, Shreveport, Louisiana.

37. Mitchell, who was actually a commander in the Confederate States Navy, had been given command of all naval operations in the area of the forts by William C. Whittle, commandant of the New Orleans Naval Station. *ORN,* XVIII, 323–24.

relief was not extended to him, all of his heavy guns in the Fort would soon be disabled by the enemy's fire, so that when his Fleet should attempt to engage the Fort at close quarters, or to dash past, the chances of a successful resistance would be materially & dangerously diminished.

But Capt. Mitchell resisted the importunities of Gen. Duncan and declined to remove the *Louisiana* to the designated spot. He wished to remain where he was, just above Fort St. Philip, until his vessel should be completed. [He] declared that the *Louisiana,* though having her sides well protected, was not shot proof against the vertical fire of mortars and that it would not be advisable to anchor her below the raft. His subordinate officers concurred with his opinion. Gen. Duncan sent a detachment of 150 picked men to work the *Louisiana*'s guns and to act as sharpshooter[s] on board. He also urged upon Capt. Mitchell the absolute necessity of keeping the River lighted up at night & of sending down fire barges against the enemy's ships.

About noon Fort St. Philip opened fire from its heaviest guns upon the enemy, with a view of dislodging his mortar boats or of drawing their fire; but they persistantly kept pounding away at Fort Jackson, now and then firing a rifle gun at St. Philip. The guns of Fort Jackson were engaged during the day in throwing shell over the Point of Woods, with apparently some effect as the mortar firing very perceptibly slackened towards afternoon. At night, however, it became furious again. While standing with Capt. [A. N.] Ogden,[38] late at night on the rampart—watching the flashing of the huge shells as they mounted towards the heavens, then turned and came rushing and screaming towards us—one shell fell very close to where we were standing. We dodged behind a gun and escaped the flying piece[s] of iron and brick that followed the explosion, but a poor fellow who had just been returned from duty & was standing near us had both legs cut off by a fragment of the shell & died in a few minutes.

Between 12 & 1 o'clock, we were startled by the cry that Magazine No. 2 was on fire. The engine was brought out quickly & the whole garrison went to work to extinguish the flames. A shell had

38. Ogden was really a lieutenant of Louisiana artillery, who worked the fort's heavy guns. *Ibid.,* 279.

fallen on top of the magazine, crushing in in [sic] the sand bag traverse, setting fire to & jamming up against the door of the Magazine, the wooden frame work that supported it. The sand bags having fallen down upon the fire made it very difficult to get at and we were in imminent danger of being blown up; only a wooden door interposed between the fire and several thousand pounds of powder. The men realized that it was a life or death struggle and went to work with a will; the bags were quickly removed and a deluge of water poured upon the fire, which was soon extinguished. The door of the Magazine was found to be considerably charred; a few more minutes of delay in putting this fire out would have proved our destruction.[39] The shell that caused all this commotion also struck a member of the St. Mary's Cannoneers, (a brother of the wife of Levi Pierce, Esq., a distinguished lawyer of New Orleans);[40] crushing him into pieces and burying him out of sight. It was three days afterwards when his remains were exhumed, & so mangled & disfigured were they that they could not have been identified had it not been for the pieces of clothing that adhered to them.[41] A soldier who was standing guard at the Magazine was so terrified that he dropped his gun and fled from the Fort during the confusion caused by the fire. This man, we afterwards learned, (who was a foreigner) deserted to the enemy and gave them much valuable information concerning the condition of the Fort, strength of the garrison, etc.

April 23d. A clear, warm day. Bombardment heavy and continuous during the day, but very perceptibly decreased towards noon. This circumstance was conclusive to our minds that the mortar fleet was getting exhausted and that the enemy were about to change their mode of attack. A short time before sun-down, a small boat was discovered planting a large number of little flags on the opposite side of the River, above the Point of Woods. This was evidently done to indicate the position of the different vessels in the

---

39. Seymour reported that the men carried by hand the 30,000 pounds of powder from Magazine No. 2 and put it in Magazine No. 1. Ex-officer, "Bombardment of Forts Jackson and St. Philip," in Seymour Papers.

40. The seventy-six-year-old jurist, a former Louisiana secretary of state, was renowned as New Orleans' finest corporate lawyer. He died in 1866. Stuart Landry, *History of the Boston Club* (New Orleans, 1938), 323.

41. Fred F. Keyl was the unfortunate soldier killed by the shell. Ex-officer, "Bombardment of Forts Jackson and St. Philip," in Seymour Papers; letter to the editor, undated newspaper clipping, *ibid.*

contemplated attack by broadsides upon the Fort. Capt. Mitchell was made acquainted with this new movement of the enemy and Gen. Duncan again urged him to place the *Louisiana* below Fort St. Philip; but he declined to do so for reasons before assigned. He was then reminded of the imperative necessity of keeping the River lighted up during the night by means of fire rafts, so that any movement of the enemy's vessels could be readily detected.

At nine o'clock at night, Lt. [George] Shryrock, acting Aid to Capt. Mitchell, came ashore and communicated with General Duncan. He promised in the name of Capt. M[itchell] that the fire barges should be sent down at intervals of two hours during the remainder of the night & that the River should be well lighted just before daylight, when the attack was expected to commence. Notwithstanding these repeated solicitations on the part of the General & the positive promises of Capt. Mitchell, not one fire-barge was sent down during this night and the River remained veiled in darkness. This strange and criminal neglect to light up the River caused the enemy to change his plan of attack and await himself of the darkness to dash past the Forts. Gen. Duncan, to my certain knowledge, did everything within his power to prevent this state of things; [but] as the control of the fire-barges had been taken out of his hands, he had to rely upon Capt. Mitchell to direct their movements. Bombardment continued all night and became more furious than ever towards morning.[42]

42. While Duncan pressured Mitchell to move the *Louisiana,* General Lovell was doing the same with Whittle in New Orleans. Lovell urged Whittle to order Mitchell to move the ironclad to a position one-half mile below the raft along the east bank. There it would be protected by the forts' crossfire and could dislodge the mortar boats with its rifled guns. Whittle finally telegraphed Mitchell and suggested this, but Mitchell declined, citing his previous reasons for not doing so. Through Lieutenant Shryock, Mitchell informed Duncan that the *Louisiana* would be fully ready for action by the evening of April 24, but Duncan replied that that would probably be too late. Seymour may be mistaken in claiming that no fire rafts were used. Farragut's log claims that the *Hartford* was set afire briefly by one.

By April 23 Farragut was convinced that the two forts could not be reduced by bombardment. He had given Porter five days to make good his boast of battering them into submission with his mortar boats. Now it was time to act. Against Porter's objections, Farragut prepared his fleet to run past the forts that night.

The fleet was divided into three divisions to make the run while Porter's mortar boats remained below the forts to provide a covering fire. To prepare for the ordeal, crews draped chain armor alongside each ship to protect the engines; guns and engine rooms were sandbagged and netting was put above deck to catch falling debris. Although Farragut was confident of success, he expected to receive very heavy losses in the process.

Disorganization in the Confederate ranks greatly hindered effective opposition. Mitchell

April 24th. Long before daylight all the guns were manned, the hot shot furnaces in full blast, shot & shell placed near the guns and every preparation made for the fight. The night was intensely dark and not a breath of air stirring. At 3½ o'clock, a.m. the dim outline of the Yankee Flagship, the Sloop of War *Hartford,* was seen just above the Point of Woods. In a few minutes a red light was run up to her mast head, which was the signal to the squadron to advance. At this time the bombardment was carried on by the Mortar Fleet with terrific vigor and rapidity, as many as twelve 13 inch shells being by actual count in the air at the same time. Following the *Hartford* came the remaining vessels of Farragut's steam fleet—twenty-three in number[43]—advancing in column of twos in echelon, so as not to interfere with the fire of each other's broadsides. These vessels had a full head of steam on and rushed up the River with great rapidity. As soon as they were within range, the guns of both forts opened a well directed fire upon the leading ships, which was followed by broadsides after broadsides and the engagement became general. Unfortunately the air was so still that after our first fire, the smoke hung so low over the River as to shut out the enemy's ships from our view, so that our gunners had to direct their fire by the flashes of the enemy's broadsides. At this time twenty-one mortar vessels and twenty-three Steamers, mounting in all about 200 guns, were pouring into the Forts a perfect storm of shot, shell, grape, Cannister and spherical can. The roar of the artillery was deafening; the rushing sound of the descending bombs; the sharp, whizzing noise made by the jagged fragments of exploded shells, the whir-

<hr />

supposedly commanded all vessels on the river, but he was a regular Confederate naval officer. The skippers of the River Defense Fleet were state officers and claimed to recognize no authority except that of the governor of Louisiana and the Confederate secretary of war. As a result, there was no cooperation among the boat captains, and the River Defense Fleet ignored all warnings to prepare for a possible attack. Duncan wrote later, "Unable to govern themselves, and unwilling to be governed by others, their almost total want of system, vigalence, and discipline, rendered them nearly useless and helpless when the enemy finally dashed upon them."

After midnight Lovell sailed to the forts to move the *Louisiana* to a position below the forts. The night was exceptionally dark and misty, with a chill in the air. The general arrived at approximately 2:00 A.M. and found the Confederate fleet at anchor alongside each bank with engines down. Just then, Farragut's attack began and Lovell was forced to retreat back to New Orleans to avoid capture. *ORN,* XVIII, 255, 268; Winters, *Civil War in Louisiana,* 86–93; Pratt, *Civil War on Western Waters,* 45.

43. There actually were only seventeen ships in the attack. Pratt, *Civil War on Western Waters,* 45.

ring of grape shot & hissing of Cannister balls—all this was well calculated to disturb the equanimity of the strongest nerved man, provided he was not too much engaged to allow his mind to dwell upon them, which was the case with most of us.

A lurid glow of light rested upon the Fort, produced by the almost incessant discharges of our own guns, and the explosion of the enemy's shell[s] above and around us. At one time when the din & tumult were at the highest, as I was standing at my post, Father Nachon,[44] a Catholic Priest who was volunteer Chaplain at the Fort, placed his mouth to my ear & called out that hell could not be more terrible to the sight than Fort Jackson. I was not disposed to dispute with him on that point. I will here remark, parathetically, that this good man displayed remarkable coolness and courage during the trying scenes of the bombardment; he animated the men by his eloquence and example, and won the respect of everyone by the unvarying faithfulness with which he discharged his religious duties.

With daylight came the mortifying discovery that several of the Yankee ships had succeeded in passing the Forts. Thirteen vessels had run the gauntlet and nine had been driven back.[45] As soon as we could see, we discovered one steamer below Fort St. Philip; crippled and floating down with the current, and not a man to be seen on her decks. A large double-banked frigate (sailing vessel), towed by a steamboat, attempted to pass the Forts, but our guns forced her to take shelter behind the Point of Woods. During this action the officers & men of the Forts had displayed great coolness, steadiness & bravery, remaining at their guns during one of the severest bombardments of modern times, and performing their whole duty like soldiers and patriots. They exhorted the highest praise even from their victorious enemies—it was the opinion of everyone within the Forts, that had Gen. Duncan's request been complied with by Capt. Mitchell and the River sufficiently lighted up to enable us to see to fire with accuracy, not one of the enemy's vessels would have succeeded in passing. As it was, the *Hartford* was struck thirty-one

44. Father Nachon, whose full name is unknown, was a Jesuit priest from New Orleans who served as a volunteer chaplain to the fort's garrison. He died in 1867 from yellow fever. Ex-officer, "Bombardment of Forts Jackson and St. Philip," in Seymour Papers.

45. In fact, only three of the seventeen ships in the attack failed to pass the forts. Winters, *Civil War in Louisiana*, 93.

times and set on fire twice by hot shot.[46] The Yankees' ships had
their machinery protected by heavy chain cables, hung on festoons
along the sides of the vessels amidships, and, running on an even
Keel in smooth water, it was impossible to get a shot into them
under the water line.

Our River Fleet had been moored on either side of the River just
above the Forts to be in readiness to attack the Yankee squadron
should it succeed in passing up. Immediately after the passings of
the Forts, heavy firing was heard from up the River, which continued for about one hour. Then the wrecks of several of our cotton-
clad steamers floated past us & we knew that our little fleet had
yielded to the superior weight & numbers of the enemy. The *Manassas* (iron-clad ram) was seen having an unequal combat with the
Steam Frigate *Mississippi,* whose heavy guns fired at short-range
tore great holes in the sides of our little iron-clad; still her gallant
commander, Capt. Warley, persevered in fighting and tried his best
to sink his formidable opponent by running into her. This he failed
to do, owing to his inferior motive power. He afterwards made an
effort to run into the *Richmond* (of 24 guns)[47] and was just about to
accomplish his object when one of our disabled cotton-clads came
in between the hostile ships, forcing him to sheer off, and the *Manassas* missed her mark & fell astern of the *Richmond.* Finding that
his vessel was settling fast, he ran her ashore and escaped with his
crew.[48] The last of our vessels to give up the unequal contest was the
McRae. Her brave Captain (Huger) had been mortally wounded,
but his first officer, [Lt. Charles W. Read], continued to fight her.
When we saw her contending with two of the enemy's large Steam

---

46. The log of Farragut's flagship makes no mention of the number of hits it sustained or
of being hit with hotshot, although it was briefly set aflame by a fire raft. *ORN,* XVIII,
719–20.

47. The USS *Richmond* actually had thirty guns. *Ibid.,* 690.

48. The *Manassas* was one of the few Confederate boats that actively fought the Union
fleet. Intended originally as a privateer, the converted tug was fitted with armor, ram, and
armament but at only four knots proved too slow as a raider. When Farragut raced past the
forts, the *Manassas* put one shell through the USS *Brooklyn,* but low steam pressure caused
her ram to bounce off the *Brooklyn's* armor. Then, swapping blows with the USS *Mississippi,*
Captain Warley knocked his foe aground temporarily, only later to be run aground himself
by the *Mississippi.* The *Manassas* was then raked with two broadsides from the *Mississippi* and
exploded soon after the crew abandoned her. Winters, *Civil War in Louisiana,* 92; Pratt, *Civil
War on Western Waters,* 35–36.

sloops, we gave her a rousing cheer by way of encouragement & applause. At last she was forced to retire under cover of the Forts.

Some five or six miles above us, a running fight had been going on for almost an hour between two of our steamers, the *Gov. Moore,* Capt. Beverly Kennon, and the *Genl. Quitman,* Capt. Alex Grant—and the Yankee Steam Sloop *Varuna.* The *Quitman* ran into the *Varuna* once, but did not sink her, when she was driven off by other vessels & set on fire. The fight was kept up most gallantly by Kennon; one of his guns (he had only two on board) was disabled & two-thirds of his men killed or wounded.[49] Finding that he could not continue this unequal conflict much longer, the gallant Kennon determined to run his antagonist down. So after skillfully maneuvring he got his prow directed towards the *Varuna,* in doing which he was subjected to a terrible raking fire from the enemy's 11 & 9 inch Dalgren guns, and putting on all steam he struck her on the quarter, sinking her in ten minutes. The Yankee guns kept firing until the water reached the spar deck and succeeded in disabling the engines of the *Gov. Moore.* His vessel being crippled and totally unmanageable, Kennon set fire to her to prevent her from falling into the enemy's hands, and surrendered to one of the Yankee vessels that came to the service of the *Varuna.* Much credit was deservedly awarded to Capt. Kennon for the skill and courage he displayed in this action. The *Gov. Moore* was a large sea-steamer that had be[en] converted into a war steamer by means of cotton bulkheads; she mounted two guns—old thirty-two pounders that had been rifled. The *Varuna* carried nine guns of the heaviest calibre and was altogether a splendid steam sloop-of-war.[50]

One of our steamers, the *Resolute,* was run ashore about a mile above the Forts, where she displayed a white flag in token of surrender; but an officer & a boat's crew boarded her from the *McRae,* hauled down her flag & fought her only serviceable gun until they were obliged to destroy her to prevent capture.[51]

The *McRae, Louisiana* & *Defiance* were the only vessels that escaped destruction; the *Louisiana* having remained at her anchorage

49. Of his ninety-three crewmen, Kennon lost fifty-seven dead and seventeen wounded. Winters, *Civil War in Louisiana,* 94.

50. The USS *Varuna* mounted eight 8-inch howitzers and two 30-pound cannons. *ORN,* XVIII, 690.

51. Lieutenant Thomas Arnold and ten crewmen performed this heroic duty. *Ibid.,* 333.

just above Fort St. Philip. None of the remaining vessels fell into the hands of the enemy, all of them having been destroyed by their commanders when they found that they could not cope with the powerful batteries of the enemy.[52] It was a sad & discouraging spectacle that these wrecks presented as they floated past the Forts shortly after daylight. I have forgotten to mention that [the] C[onfederate] S[tates] Steamer *Jackson*, Capt. Renshaw, which was stationed at the Quarantine when the firing between the fleets commenced after the passage of the Forts steamed up the River with unseemly haste, making one of the quickest trips to New Orleans on record and being the first to convey to the city the unwelcome tidings of our discomfiture—its commander showing far greater aptitude for a news messenger than for a brave fighter.

On board of the *Louisiana* we lost a number of [the] best & bravest men in killed & wounded belonging to the detachments from the Forts, while her immediate commander, Capt. McIntosh, was so severely wounded that he died a few days after. His conduct was most highly spoken of by all who witnessed his courageous bearing on that occasion.

The enemy's fleet above the Forts captured Col. [I.] Szymanski's Regiment of Infantry stationed there [at the Quarantine], and at 10 o'clock a.m. eleven of their vessels steamed slowly towards the City, leaving two gunboats behind to keep watch over us and to cover the landing of troops at the Quarantine from the bay back of the Station. These boats came down to the point one mile & a half above the Forts to reconnoitre, but did not attempt to molest our fatigue parties who were busily engaged in repairing damages and making preparations to resist attacks from above and below. On this day a gunboat from below made her appearance with a flag of truce flying at the fore and demanded the surrender of the Forts, threatening, in the name of Commodore D[avid] D[ixon] Porter, to re-open the bombardment in case of refusal. The proposition was respectfully declined and at noon the mortar vessels, which had been dumb since the passage of the Forts, recommenced their infer-

---

52. The USS *Cayuga* singlehandedly destroyed most of the River Defense Fleet. She steamed far ahead of her sister ships, driving the Confederate gunboats ashore, where they were burned. The rest of the Confederate boats, with the exception of the *Manassas*, *Governor Moore*, and *McRae*, put up a poor fight and were easily dispatched by the federals. *Ibid.*, 269; Pratt, *Civil War on Western Waters*, 89.

nal noise & kept up a languid fire until sunset, when they hauld up their anchors and sailed down the River, much to our joy & relief. Six gunboats remained behind the Point of Woods.[53]

April 25th. No attack from the enemy during the day; the two gunboats above would occasionaly show their noses around the point to gratify their Yankee curiosity and discover what we were about. Men & officers hard at work making needed repairs to the Forts. We all were under the impression that the severest fighting was yet to come and diligently addressed ourselves to the task of preparing for it.

The enemy granted permission to the *McRae* to proceed to New Orleans with the wounded of both Forts—which she accordingly did. She was so badly crippled that she could be of no service to us; she went up under a flag of truce. Just before she started I went aboard to express to Capt. Tom Huger my heart-felt sympathy for him in his wounded condition; found him much prostrated by his wounds, which were very severe, and much dispirited by the success of the Yankees. (Poor fellow, he died a few weeks afterwards). The *McRae* never returned to the Forts, but sunk at the levee at New Orleans during the weeks after her departure.

April 26. Capt. Mitchell communicated with the enemy above [the forts] under flag of truce; they informed him that New Orleans had surrendered, which was false, and was no doubt fabricated for the purpose of deceiving and disheartening the garrison of the Forts.[54] They also gave us information of the burning by our authorities of the C[onfederate] S[tates] Steam Ram *Mississippi,* which we subsequently found to be true. This vessel was one of the strongest and most powerful iron clads ever constructed, and had she been completed in time to participate in the fight at the Forts, I have no doubt that the issue would have been different. The work on her was carried on so slowly that to many persons of judgement and experience in ship-building there was an unmistakable appearance of a design on the part of her constructors, the Messrs. [N. and A. F. Tift] Tiffts, to delay her completion. Be this as it may, I know

53. Porter withdrew the mortar boats to be refitted and to be in a safer position in case the *Louisiana* ventured downriver. *ORN*, XVIII, 369.

54. Seymour is splitting hairs here. Although it is true that New Orleans did not formally surrender until April 29, Farragut captured the city on April 25 and raised the U.S. flag over the U.S. Mint the next day. Winters, *Civil War in Louisiana,* 95–96.

that there was a great lack of energy displayed in the building of this vessel and that at a time when an attack upon the Forts was hourly expected, and the strongest representations had been made that the services of the *Mississippi* were needed, no work was done on her during the night.[55]

About noon we noticed a large Frigate & several transports in the bay back of Fort St. Philip. Later we discried [?] a steamboat making her way up the bay, evidently trying to reach the mouth of the bayou that led to the Quarantine Station.[56]

April 27. At daylight the Steamer that had been seen the day before was discovered in the bay at the mouth of Fort Bayou immediately in the rear of Fort St. Philip; some twelve ships' launches were near her, engaged in landing troops at the Quarantine above us. At 12 o'clock. M., a gunboat appeared around the Point of Woods below us bearing a flag of truce; a small boat was sent to meet her, when it was found that she bore a written document from Commodore Porter for us to surrender. The Commodore complimented, in the most flattering terms, the gallantry displayed by [our] officers and men in the defence of the Forts; announced that the City of New Orleans had surrendered to Commodore Farragut (which was a Yankee lie)—declared that it would lead to a useless expenditure of life to attempt a further defence of the Forts; and offered us the most favorable terms if we would capitulate.[57] This demand was met by a positive declination on the part of our Commander, who declared his intentions to defend the Forts so long as his men would stand by him.

Throughout the bombardment and the action of the morning of the 24th, the conduct of the men was admirable; they had proved

---

55. N. and A. F. Tift began building the *Mississippi* in October, 1861. But the Confederate government took away most of the city's skilled labor for other projects, and it was difficult to get the material needed to complete the ship. After the builders worked day and night, the *Mississippi* was finally launched unfinished because public outcry demanded it. Although this was frustrating, there is no evidence to support Seymour's belief that intrigue was involved. *ORN,* XVIII, 331; John Smith Kendall, *History of New Orleans* (3 vols.; Chicago, 1922), I, 244.

56. Porter sent two schooners to the rear of Fort St. Philip and six behind Fort Jackson to cut off the forts' supply and escape routes. By the morning of April 27 both forts were completely surrounded. *ORN,* XVIII, 331.

57. Porter offered to allow the Confederate officers to keep their sidearms in return for the garrisons' pledge not to take up arms again until properly exchanged. In addition, the forts, cannons, muskets, ammunition, and provisions were to be surrendered undamaged. *Ibid.,* 369.

themselves excellent soldiers—brave in battle, obedient to orders—and had displayed remarkable energy and constancy in the performance of their arduous and protracted labors. While under the excitement of actual conflict they manifested a cheerful, confident and an enthusiastic spirit; but after the enemy's ships had effected the passage of the Forts, they became surly and despondent, which was not surprising when we take into consideration that they were for the most part foreigners and men of very low moral status. Gen. Duncan attempted to arouse their flagging zeal by issuing to them a spirited address, exhorting them to keep up their courage, and in this hour of trial, to act like soldiers and patriots; but it had no perceptible effect, except upon the members of the "St. Mary's Cannoniers" who were of the better class of men and were "to the manor born."[58]

Late in the day a laundress attached to one of our companies, who had been sent to the Quarantine just before the bombardment commenced, returned to the Fort, and though she was not permitted to come on shore, she managed to inform one of our pickets that the City had certainly surrendered to Commodore Farragut. This intelligence, which had no foundation in fact, spread quickly through the garrison and produced a most dispiriting effect upon the men. About 11 o'clock P.M. the men at a given signal fell into line on the parade plein, under command of their Sergeants, with loaded muskets; they were commanded by their commissioned officers to go to their quarters, which they positively refused to do, declaring at the same time that they would fight no longer. In explanation of their conduct, these men stated that they knew that Genl. Duncan was resolved to fight as long as the provisions lasted and then blow up the Forts and everything in them; that the City had capitulated and that there was no further use in fighting; that the enemy were about to attack by land and water on three sides at once, and that a longer defence would only prove a butchery.

Every effort was made by the officers to induce the mutineers to return to duty; of course force could not be used, for the officers only numbered thirty-seven, while there were about four hundred

58. The St. Mary's Cannoneers, a company largely made up of planters' sons, was organized by Captain F. O. Cornay in December, 1861, in St. Mary Parish. John Dimitry, *Louisiana* (Atlanta, 1899), 322e, Vol. X of Clement Evans, ed., *Confederate Military History,* 10 vols.

men engaged in the mutiny. The St. Mary's Cannoniers were quartered outside of the Fort; the mutineers had attempted by threats to force them to join them, but they refused to participate in the disgraceful revolt. That the Cannoniers might not come to the assistance of the officers within the Fort, the draw bridge was raised, a strong guard placed at the sally-port, and all communication from without effectually cut off. A strong party went up on the ramparts and spiked the guns that bore up the river to prevent us, as they said afterwards, from firing upon them after they had left the Fort. Some of our officers endeavored to put a stop to this, when they were fired upon, but without effect. Father Nachon, Dr. Burke & myself went among the men, represented to them the disgrace & dishonor they were bringing upon themselves, and entreated them to return to duty. A large number were prevailed upon to go to their quarters, but not until the promise had been exacted from us that the mutineers who still held out should be permitted to leave the Fort unmolested. Accordingly about two hundred and fifty men, with arms in their hands, marched out & proceeded up the River; among them were men from every company within the Fort and many who had distinguished themselves by their cool bravery and strict adherence to duty during the bombardment.[59]

The mutineers having carried away all of the small boats, we could not communicate with Fort St. Philip and were consequently kept in ignorance of the state of affairs over there. It soon became apparent that but little reliance could be placed in the broken detachments that remained to defend the Fort; one company, it is true, remained intact, the "St. Mary's Cannoniers," but they had been drilled in light artillery and knew nothing about the working of heavy guns. It would be impossible for us to strengthen the garrison at Fort Jackson by drawing men from Fort St. Philip, for in the expected combined land and water attack, the latter, from its position, would inevitably be the point attacked by the enemy's land force and would require all of its garrison to repel the assault. Such being the condition of affairs, it was the unanimous opinion of

59. Apparently the lack of action since the twenty-fourth gave the men time to reflect on their situation and to concoct the rumor of Duncan's purported plan to blow up the fort. The mutiny caught the officers completely off guard, and the 250 men involved later surrendered to federal troops near the Quarantine. Winters, *Civil War in Louisiana*, 100–101.

the officers of Fort Jackson that there was no other course left to us but to surrender and it was resolved to open negotiations for that purpose early next morning, in order to obtain from Commodore Porter, before he had received information of the mutiny and of our crippled condition, the honorable terms that he had offered on the previous day, and which had been declined.

April 28th. Shortly after daylight Capt. [M. T.] Squires, Commanding at Fort St. Philip, Capt. [Richard C.] Bond & Lieut. [Joseph K.] Dixon[60] of the Regular Army, came across the River and concurred with us that nothing was left but to surrender; at the same time declaring that they were not at all confident of the loyalty of their own troops, after the unexpected revolt at Fort Jackson—though they had not as yet showed any mutinous inclination.

Capt. Mitchell also came ashore and made an unusual exhibition of combative energy, as far as his words went; suddenly he displayed an exceedingly aggressive disposition and declared his intention to immediately attack, with the *Louisiana,* the gunboats lying at Quarantine. This struck us as being a remarkable resolve on the Captain's part, for on the previous day he had asserted that the *Louisiana* could not be moved to a position just above Fort Jackson, only a few hundred yds. from his anchorage, which Gen. Duncan had requested him to assume [so] that his vessel might more effectively assist in repelling the contemplated attack.

A flag of truce was sent down to the Fleet below the Point of Woods to convey a written offer to surrender under the terms offered by Commodore Porter on the previous day. Soon after, the Flag ship *Harriet Lane* accompanied by four gun boats, came up to the Fort with flags flying at the fore, white flags [also] being displayed from the yards of the flag masts of both Forts. Gen. Duncan and Lt. Col. Higgins went aboard the *[Harriet] Lane* and opened negociations for the surrender. While these proceedings were going on, the *Louisiana* was discovered to be on fire; her guns, which protruded from her port holes, went off at random, each being discharged as the fire reached [it]. A few minutes afterwards a deafen-

---

60. Captain M. T. Squires, of the 1st Louisiana Artillery, commanded Fort St. Philip; Captain Richard C. Bond was with the 1st Louisiana Artillery; and Lieutenant Joseph K. Dixon commanded a company of Confederate States regulars at Fort St. Philip. *ORN,* XVIII, 273; Ex-officer, "Bombardment of Forts Jackson and St. Philip," in Seymour Papers.

ing report was heard, which was followed by a huge column of smoke that ascended towards the heavens; fragments of wood and iron fell in all directions, some of them falling within Fort St. Philip, killing one of our men and wounding three others. A large piece of iron struck a tent in which was lying Capt. McIntosh, who had been terribly wounded on the *Louisiana* in the action of the morning of the 24th inst.; fortunately he escaped without further injury.[61]

The terms of surrender were soon agreed upon; the officers & men were allowed to retire upon their parole of honor that they would not take up arms against the United States until they were regularly exchanged; the officers were to retain their side arms, and all private property to be respected. Commodore Porter orally agreed not to haul down the Confederate flag or hoist the Federal flag until the officers should have left the Forts. About 3 o'clock in the afternoon the officers of Fort Jackson and the "St. Mary's Cannoniers" left for New Orleans on board the gunboat *Kennebic*. The surrender of Fort Jackson was a sad spectacle and tears came freely from the eyes of officers and men who had never flinched during all the trying scenes of one of the severest bombardments of modern times.[62]

From the morning of the morning [sic] of the 18th to the evening of the 23d of April, over *twelve thousand 13 inch mortar shells* were thrown at Fort Jackson; of which *seven thousand five hundred and thirty-seven* fell within the confines of the Fort.[63] When we consider the severity of the bombardment, the casualties in Fort Jackson were remarkably few in number: killed 16, wounded 69.[64]

61. Porter had just demanded that Mitchell be present at the negotiations when the *Louisiana* drifted by in flames. Mitchell, not being under army command, decided to destroy the *Louisiana* rather than surrender her. Porter claimed that Mitchell intended for the ship to blow up inside the federal fleet and labeled him "the archtraitor." Mitchell and all of the Confederate naval officers were subsequently arrested and sent to prison in retaliation for the *Louisiana* incident. *ORN,* XVIII, 370–71; Winters, *Civil War in Louisiana,* 100–101.

62. Porter saw the surrender differently: "The sun never shone on a more contented and happy looking set of faces than those of the prisoners. . . . They emerged from the fort . . . like a parcel of happy schoolboys in holiday times." *ORN,* XVIII, 371.

63. Porter wrote that Confederate prisoners estimated 3,000 shells hit the fort. He claimed that 1,800 fell within the fort, while many others hit around it or exploded overhead. *Ibid.,* 372, 437.

64. Other sources place losses in Fort Jackson at 9 dead and 33 wounded. Fort St. Philip lost 2 dead and 4 wounded and the Confederate navy 74 dead and 75 wounded. Farragut reported his casualties as 39 dead and 171 wounded. *Ibid.,* 284; Winters, *Civil War in Louisiana,* 98.

The enemy occasionally threw into the Fort shells filled with a peculiar chemical compound which, when it exploded, emitted a most disgusting odor—one that could not be paralleled except by the combined stench of the "sixty-seven well defined stinks of Cologne." One night whilst several of us who were off duty at the time were quietly sleeping in a casemate, one of these shells exploded at the door, filling the apartment with a most stifling and offensive smoke. Dr. Bradbury quickly awakened and warned us to go out immediately into the fresh air or else we would die of asphyxia; we acted upon his advice instanter and thus were fairly smoked out of our quarters.[65]

During the action of the morning of the 24th inst. some of the enemy's vessels, after passing the Forts were guilty of the diabolical inhumanity of firing into the houses of peacably inoffensive citizens situated on the banks of the River. At the door of one of these houses was standing a young girl watching the progress of the Federal fleet up the River; one of the ships fired a shot at the house which severed the girl's head from her body. She was the daughter of an old U.S. Ordnance Sargeant who had had charge of the Forts before they were seized by the state troops, and who had since adhered to the Federal cause.[66]

April 29th. At 11 o'clock a.m. we arrived at New Orleans. Gen. Duncan and I were the first to land and were met on the levee by a large and excited crowd, who at first took us for Federal officers and looked as if disposed to offer us violence. In a few moments, however, some persons recognized us, whereupon we were cheered most lustily; they assured us that they believed that we had done our whole duty at the Forts and congradulated us upon our escape from personal injury during the bombardment. I accompanied the General to the City Hall where he went to report to the Mayor of the City; the State flag being the only one that was flying in New Orleans, the Confederate authorities having left. On our way thither we were accompanied by a very large crowd of people, who in the most demonstrative manner, manifested their good feeling for us

---

65. There is no evidence that federal gunners used any gaseous shells.

66. This incident is not mentioned in any New Orleans newspapers or other records, but the federals did shell the Chalmette area on April 25, and the killing could have occurred there. Kendall, *History of New Orleans,* I, 262.

and their approbation of our course. [When we] arrived at the Hall, the Mayor [John T.] Monroe made a speech to Gen. Duncan in which he expressed the highest admiration for the manner in which the Genl. & his officers had conducted themselves during the bombardment, and assured him that it was the opinion of the people of New Orleans that he had done all that brave man and skilful soldier could do for the defence of the Forts. The Hon. Pierre Soulé[67] addressed him in similar language and sentiment to which he made a suitable response.

At this time the Yankee ships lying in the River abreast of the city had their guns bearing upon the principle streets running diagnally with the River. Commodore Farragut had demanded the surrender of the city and had threatened that if his demand was met by a refusal, he would proceed to bombard the city. At first the Mayor declined to surrender and several hundreds of ladies signed a petition in which they exhorted him to hold out, and expressed their willingness to encounter all the sufferings and dangers of a bombardment, rather than have their beloved city surrendered to the enemy. But at last more prudent counsels prevailed and the city was virtually, though not formally, surrendered; the enemy being allowed to come ashore unmolested and raise the U.S. flag over the Government buildings. Previously [April 26] Farragut had sent an armed detachment ashore and raised the "Stars & Stripes" over the U.S. Mint, but it was immediately hauled down and torn in tatters by a mob. A man named [William] Mumford, who was charged with being a participant in this transaction, was afterwards inhumanly hung by order of that cowardly old brute, Gen. Butler.[68]

The Yankees now became masters of the "Crescent City;" three days afterwards a large force of infantry was landed and Maj. Gen. B. F. Butler, appositely named and universally known as "Beast Butler," became Military Governor. His brutish instincts, cruel tyr-

67. Pierre Soulé was a prominent Louisiana politician who had served both as a state senator and U.S. senator. Before the war he had championed states' rights and now served as the provost marshal for New Orleans. He later was arrested by Butler and deported from the state. Dumas Malone, ed., *Dictionary of American Biography* (20 vols.; New York, 1928–36), XVII, 405–407.

68. William Mumford led a crowd of protesters to the U.S. Mint on April 26 and tore down the U.S. flag. His execution made Mumford one of the South's most famous martyrs. Winters, *Civil War in Louisiana*, 98, 134.

anny and barbarous treatment of the citizens of New Orleans (both men and women) during his administration have consigned his name to eternal infamy.[69]

Most of the officers who had been paroled at the surrender of the Forts—myself included—remained in New Orleans, our home, waiting to be exchanged. Shortly after his accession to power, Butler issued an order for the government of the Press of the City.[70] It was purposely couched in ambiguious language and the members of the "Associated Press," of which I was President, had a meeting and appointed three members—Messrs. Alex Walker, John Magimsis & the writer—to wait on Gen. Butler and demand an explanation. The interview was quite an interesting one, many spicy things having been said on both sides, but we got little or no satisfaction from the old "Beast." In course of the conversation I asked old Butler what would be the result if he were to issue a General Order which would be in conflict with the laws of war and [illegible] of nations, and I were to criticize it and show wherein it conflicted with those laws and [illegible]. He told me, in reply, that nothing would excuse me in pursuing such a course; declaring that his authority as Military Governor was supreme, and that the propriety and legality of his acts and edicts could not be questioned—that to do so would be an unpardonable sin "like sinning against the Holy Ghost"—a more impious and blasphemous distinction never fell from human lips.[71]

Butler having informed me that if I closed my office (of the N[ew] O[rleans] *Commercial Bulletin*) he would seize it & make it a Union paper, I resolved to publish it until I should be exchanged, when I intended to abandon my paper and rejoin the Confederate

69. Butler commanded an occupation army of eighteen thousand and ruled with an iron fist. His tenure was marked by massive arrests of civilians and rumors of bribery and theft on the part of Butler and his brother. When Mayor John Monroe protested the excesses, he was summarily removed from office. But it was Butler's infamous "Women's Order," which called for women who insulted Union soldiers to be treated as prostitutes, that primarily earned him the nickname "Beast." *Ibid.*, 125–48.

70. Butler launched a ruthless campaign to bring the vocal rebel papers of New Orleans under control. After issuing a censorship proclamation, the *Daily True Delta, Bee, Daily Delta, Crescent,* and *Picayune* were all closed or seized by federal troops for various infractions. *Ibid.*, 131.

71. Seymour later wrote that Butler "raged like a mad bull" at his impudence. He pounded his desk and roared, "I am the military Governor of this State—the Supreme Power—you cannot disregard my order, sir. By God, he that sins against me, sins against the Holy Ghost." Ex-officer, "Bombardment of Forts Jackson and St. Philip," in Seymour Papers.

Army. I continued to publish my paper, in opposition to the policy of the U.S. Government, until the 28th day of July. On the 27th of that month I rec'd a confirmation that my Dear Father had been killed in battle in Virginia.[72] On the next morning I published a biographical sketch of him to which my commercial editor, Mr. J. C. Dinnies, made an addition; in the last paragraph [he] declared that Father, in the Florida, Mexican & Confederate wars, had been actuated by the purist and most patriotic of motives—a sense of duty. Butler pretended to find something very treasonable in his expression and sent one of his Staff Officers with a guard of twenty-five men to my office, bearing and [sic] order for the arrest of Mr. Dinnies & me. We were consequently taken to the Custom House & placed in *durance vile.*

On the following day Butler published an order confiscating my property, revoking my parole & consigning me to close confinement at Fort Jackson until further orders. Gen. [Godfrey] Weitzel and other members of his Staff told Butler that he could not legally revoke my parole, since he did not charge me with having broken it & that if he considered me a dangerous character, he could only send me beyond his lines. The old Beast said in reply that he did not care whether he was acting according to was acting under [sic] military laws or not—that he intended putting me in prison and should do so immediately. On the 1st of August I was placed in confinement at Fort Jackson, where I remained until the 17th of October.[73] On that day I came up to New Orleans for the purpose of going on a Flag of Truce boat to Vicksburg to be exchanged; but through the tardiness of Brig. Genl. Neal Dow (of Maine Signor law notoriety)[74] who Commanded the two Forts, the order for my release was not delivered in time to enable me to reach the City before the boat left for Vicksburg.

Butler paroled me, giving me the freedom of the city and prom-

72. Colonel Isaac G. Seymour was killed on June 27, 1862, at the Battle of Gaines' Mill while temporarily commanding the 1st Louisiana Brigade. Terry L. Jones, *Lee's Tigers: The Louisiana Infantry in the Army of Northern Virginia* (Baton Rouge, 1987), 103.

73. Dinnies was also imprisoned with Seymour. Seymour obituary, November 11, 1886, newspaper clipping, in Seymour Papers.

74. General Neal Dow was a famous temperance supporter before and during the war. He was colonel of the 13th Maine Volunteers before being given command of Forts Jackson and St. Philip. Ezra J. Warner, *Generals in Blue: Lives of the Union Commanders* (Baton Rouge, 1964), 130–31.

ised to give me a passport to go beyond the Yankee lines by the first flag of truce boat. Notwithstanding this promise, the old "Beast" would not permit me to go, though I made repeated demands for a passport, until the 14th of December, when I crossed Lake Pontchartrain and landed at Mandeville. Thence I proceeded to Richmond. On my way to that place I stopped at Knoxville, Tennessee, to see Gen. Duncan, but found upon my arrival, to my unexpressible sorrow, that he had died the day previously.[75]

At Richmond Col. [Robert] Ould, C[onfederate] S[tates] Agent of Exchange, gave me a certificate of exchange & the Secretary of War granted me a leave of absence for 60 days. I visited Vicksburg and was present during the first engagement with the Yankee gunboats;[76] while there a dispatch informed me that my wife, whom I had married on the 27th of October 1862, while a prisoner of war in New Orleans, had come out into the Confederacy to join me. I escorted her to Georgia (Macon) for the purpose of getting her a "local habitation" while I was absent in the army.

75. After being exchanged, Duncan was appointed chief of staff for General Braxton Bragg but died of fever at Knoxville on December 18, 1862. Warner, *Generals in Gray*, 77–78.

76. Seymour is apparently referring to the December 27–29, 1862, battle at Chickasaw Bluffs. A combined Union force of infantry and gunboats commanded by William T. Sherman and David D. Porter, respectively, attempted to take the high ground along the Yazoo River northeast of Vicksburg. After a naval bombardment, the infantry assaulted the bluffs but was severely defeated by the Confederate defenders. Faust, *Encyclopedia of the Civil War*, 138–39.

THE CAMPAIGN IN VIRGINIA

EYMOUR'S initiation into combat had been arduous, but he had met the challenge. His actions at Fort Jackson drew praise from Duncan, and New Orleans newspapers spoke highly of him. Furthermore, his harsh treatment at the hands of Butler and his refusal to be intimidated also earned him accolades.[1] With his father dead and the family newspaper confiscated, nothing now kept Seymour from fulfilling his wish to join the army. Upon release from his confinement at Fort Jackson, Seymour wrote Brigadier General Harry T. Hays, Richard Taylor's successor as commander of the 1st Louisiana Brigade. Explaining how Duncan's death had left him without a position, Seymour inquired if Hays might have a place for him on his staff. Seymour was eager to rejoin the war, and his letter flowed with praise: "Though well acquainted with a large number of the General officers in our Army, I have not applied to one of them for a position, preferring, if possible, to be with you—Louisiana's favorite General."[2] The flattery apparently worked, for Seymour was promptly offered a position as Hays's volunteer aide.

Hays was a rising star among Robert E. Lee's commanders. Born in Wilson County, Tennessee, on April 14, 1820, Hays was orphaned early in life and was raised by an uncle in Wilkinson County, Mississippi. After receiving an education at Baltimore's St. Mary's College, he moved to New Orleans and began practicing law and making a name for himself within the Whig party. As a prominent member of New Orleans society and a Mexican War veteran, he was quickly elected colonel of the 7th Louisiana Volunteers when the Civil War began. Hays soon became known as a hard-fighting, hard-drinking officer. Serving in Richard Taylor's 1st Louisiana Brigade, Hays saw much action in Jackson's Valley Campaign and

---

1. Ex-officer, "Bombardment of Forts Jackson and St. Philip," in Seymour Collection; *ORN*, XVIII, 275.

2. William J. Seymour to Harry T. Hays, January 23, 1863, in Compiled Service Records of Confederate General and Staff Officers, War Record Group 109, Microcopy 331, Roll 223, National Archives.

was severely wounded at Port Republic. When Taylor was promoted to major general and transferred to the Trans-Mississippi Department, he recommended that Hays be promoted to brigadier general and take over the 1st Louisiana Brigade.[3]

Hays received his promotion on July 25, 1862, but because of his wound did not rejoin the brigade until the Battle of Antietam. His initiation as brigade commander was a nightmare—in thirty minutes of combat at Antietam he lost over half his men. But the brigade had withstood the slaughter and fulfilled all that was required of it. It fared better during the December battle at Fredericksburg, where it was only lightly engaged.[4]

For several months after the winter battle, Lee remained encamped along the Rappahannock River at Fredericksburg. By early 1863, Hays's brigade was well known in the Virginia army. It consisted of the 5th, 6th, 7th, 8th, and 9th Louisiana Volunteers and was part of Richard Ewell's division in Stonewall Jackson's 2nd Corps. The brigade participated in all of the major campaigns and earned a reputation as one of Lee's most dependable units. But it was perhaps even more famous for its behavior off the battlefield. With a large number of swarthy foreigners, a habit of using French drill commands, and a disposition for wild, erratic behavior, the 1st Louisiana Brigade was popularly known as the notorious Louisiana Tigers. While encamped at Hamilton's Crossing on the extreme right of Lee's line at Fredericksburg, Hays waged a relentless battle against brigade members who were regularly pillaging local farms. It was a never-ending struggle and often led to clashes with Hays's superior, Major General Jubal Early, who temporarily commanded Ewell's division.[5]

When Seymour joined Hays's staff in the spring of 1863, the brigade was emerging from a dismal winter of food shortages, scant clothing, and low morale as a result of physical privations and the persistent accusations of misconduct. But spring brought a metamorphosis as warmer weather and increased camp activity lifted spirits. It was a new campaign season, and Lee's proud veterans were confident of new victories. But across the Rappahannock the federals in the Army of the Potomac were just as confident.

3. Warner, *Generals in Gray*, 130; Jones, *Lee's Tigers*, 37, 48–50, 111.

4. Jones, *Lee's Tigers*, 128–30, 143–44; Warner, *Generals in Gray*, 130.

5. Clipping from New Orleans *Times Democrat*, n.d., in Reminiscences Division, Confederate Veteran Papers, Duke University, Durham, N.C.; Order by General Harry T. Hays, December 30, 1862, in Louisiana Troops, 7th Regiment Orderly Book, 1862–64, New York Public Library, Rare Books and Manuscripts Division, New York, New York; Jones, *Lee's Tigers*, 21–44.

The humiliating December defeat under the leadership of Ambrose Burnside was behind them. Now led by the aggressive General Joseph Hooker, the Yankees had ambitious plans. Hooker's spring offensive called for General John Sedgwick to tie down Lee at Fredericksburg by crossing the river with his corps while Hooker crossed the main army far upstream. He could then sweep into Lee's rear by way of Chancellorsville and crush the rebel army. Seymour was about to witness his first large-scale infantry battle.

O N the 3d of April, 1863, I left Augusta, Ga., for Richmond, where I arrived on the 8th; thence proceeded on the 17th inst. to Hamilton's Crossing, near the town of Fredericksburg, around which the "Army of Northern Virginia," [under] Genl. Rob[er]t E. Lee, was encamped. Reaching that place the same day, at 12 o'clock, M., I found Brig. Gen. Harry T. Hays (Comdg. 1st Louisiana Brigade) awaiting my arrival with an extra horse upon which I rode to his camp, a mile distant. The General's Staff was full and I joined it as a Volunteer Aide de Camp. I had been induced to come to Virginia by a promise of Genl. H[ay]s' to make me his Adjutant General, under the new law of Congress increasing the Genl. Staff of the Army, but the bill never received the signature of the President and, consequently, failed to become a law.[6]

Our camp was situated on the sides of two hills, sheltered from the cold North winds and, though not very regularly laid out, it presented a cozy, comfortable appearance. The [men] and most of the officers lived in huts skillfully and tastefully constructed of logs, the interslices being filled with clay; but Head Quarters consisted of two large canvas tents joined together, which were far from being as comfortable as the habitations of the men. I found in the Brigade many refined, intelligent and companionable gentlemen among the officers, and as H[ead] Q[uarters] was quite a general rendezvous, I had much of their society and the time passed pleasantly. During the

---

6. Davis opposed laws allowing generals to increase their military staffs, because it deprived the president of a voice in the selection of staff officers and took too many field officers off the firing line. Wilfred Buck Yearns, *The Confederate Congress* (Athens, Ga., 1960), 108–109.

day we were occupied with drills, inspections and reviews; our evenings were spent in playing cards, singing and jovial conversation.

A short distance from camp was a high hill that commanded an extensive view of the surrounding country; to this point the General and I would often repair, with field glasses in hand, to see what the Yankees were doing on the other side of the Rappahannock. On the heights beyond the River could be seen thousands of snow-white tents and hundreds of waggons parked with the utmost regularity; the camps were swarming with our blue-coated enemies, some engaged in playing games, some in drilling, and others ranged in long, dark lines going through "dress parade" or "inspection." High above, suspended in the air, was a huge balloon from which the aernaught endeavored to reconnoitre our position and to detect any change that might be made in the disposition of our forces; but owing to the range of hills behind which our camps and movements were concealed, these aerial reconnoissances were of little or no advantage to the enemy.

Our picket lines extended along the bank of the River, while the Yankee sentinels held the opposite shore only one hundred yds. distant; notwithstanding this close proximity, the hostile lines did not fire upon each other, there being a mutual understanding that there should be no firing between pickets so long as the armies maintained their present positions. At times quite a brisk traffic was carried on between the opposing lines; logs were dug out and converted into miniature boats, to which inginiously contrived sails were fitted; these little crafts were filled with tobacco and Richmond newspapers—the only articles of traffic that our poor fellows possessed—their sails were properly trimmed to catch a favoring breese and they sped across the River with their precious freight. The Yankees would send return cargoes of many acceptable articles, but the most eagerly sought after and highly prized were coffee and sugar, which the C[onfederate] S[tates] Government was too poor to supply its soldiers with.[7]

7. Some Louisiana men even swam over to visit their foes. They found the Yankees to be as tired of the war as they were themselves, and one Tiger had a letter mailed back home to occupied Louisiana by his newly found Yankee friend. E. L. Stephens to parents, March 17, 1863, in Judge Paul Stephens Collection, Northwestern State University, Natchitoches, Louisiana; Charles Moore, Jr., Diary, March 9, 1863, Louisiana Historical Association Collection, Tulane University, New Orleans.

The enemy's position was a most advantageous one—in fact, impregnable against attack. The banks of the river on his side were, for the most part, precipitous and lofty, and "Stafford Heights"[8] afforded him many splendid positions for his artillery, which completely commanded the low, level plain that extended from the River, on our side, to the Confederate line of entrenchments, one mile broad—the same line that Burnside so unsuccessfully assaulted at the first battle of Fredericksburg. Under cover of his heavy batteries, the enemy could, at anytime and with little loss, span the River with his pontoon bridges and throw across any force he saw fit. The Confederate fortifications were situated from one thousand to twelve hundred yards from the River. On the left they ran along the crown of three high hills, called respectively Lee's & Taylor's Hills and Marye's Heights. On the right of these the line descended into and crossed a valley of two miles in breadth, until it reached a small range of hills, half a mile in length, stretching to the Railroad immediately in front of Hamilton's Crossing.

From this short and imperfect sketch of the relative positions of the two armies, it will be readily perceived that Gen. Lee was forced to keep on the defensive and that Gen. Hooker, who commanded the Federal Army, had it in his power to assume the offensive whenever he saw proper to do so. The Yankee army far outnumbered the Confederate;[9] the former were well fed, while the rations of the latter consisted of only one-third of a pound of bacon and a pound & an eighth of flour; but the *morale* of our troops was excellent, and a most [illegible] and confident feeling pervaded the ranks that our army would be victorious whenever and wherever the battle should be joined.

April 28th. This morning I visited Fredericksburg in company with Col. L[eroy] H. Stafford,[10] of the 9th La. Regt. of our Brigade,

8. Stafford Heights was a commanding ridge running parallel to the north bank of the river. Vincent J. Espisito, ed., *The West Point Atlas of American Wars* (2 vols.; New York, 1959), I, 84.

9. Hooker had approximately 115,000 men to oppose Lee's 60,000. Faust, *Encyclopedia of the Civil War,* 126.

10. Leroy Augustus Stafford was born April 13, 1822, in Rapides Parish, Louisiana. He was well educated, a successful planter, and sheriff of Rapides Parish. Stafford had volunteered for service in the Mexican War, and he opposed secession in 1861. But when war came, he organized the Stafford Guards and became lieutenant colonel of the 9th Louisiana Volunteers. When Richard Taylor was made general, Stafford was promoted to command the 9th

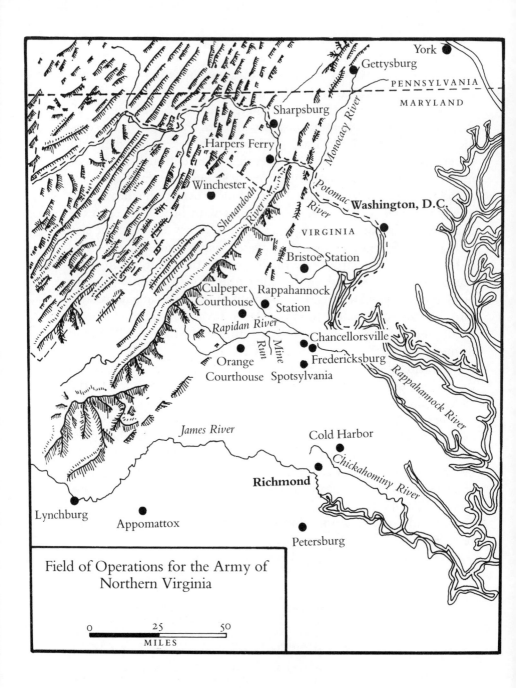

York

Gettysburg

PENNSYLVANIA
MARYLAND

Sharpsburg

Monocacy River

Harpers Ferry

Potomac

Winchester

River

Washington, D.C.

Shenandoah River

VIRGINIA

Bristoe Station

Culpeper
Courthouse

Rappahannock
Station

Rapidan River

Mine Run

Chancellorsville

Orange
Courthouse   Spotsylvania

Fredericksburg

Rappahannock River

James River

Cold Harbor

Chickahominy River

Richmond

Lynchburg

Appomattox

Petersburg

Field of Operations for the Army of
Northern Virginia

0   25   50

MILES

who was Field Officer of the day. The town presented a most dilapidated and desolate appearance; a large number of private residences were in ruins and all the Churches and public buildings were torn and battered, the effect of the shot & shell that Burnside, with the spirit of a bandal, poured upon the defenseless town at the Battle of Fredericksburg. Only a very few of the inhabitants remained—some poor whites and blacks whose scanty means would not permit them to go elsewhere.

The garrison consisted of [William] Barksdale's Brigade of Mississippians, among whom there was considerable stir and excitement owing to some unusual manifestations of activity on the part of the enemy on the other side of the river. Col. Stafford and I ascended the spire of the Episcopal Church, from which elevated position we had a fine view of the Yankee camps and forces, and a most animating & bustling sight it was. Camps were going through the process of demolition; tents were being struck, and the immense parks of waggons were unfolding themselves into long lines, whose direction could be discovered by the clouds of dust which rose from the roads they traversed. In front of this moving spectacle, and nearer the River, could be seen the hosts of the enemy, drawn up in battle array, their burnished arms glistening in the sunlight and their banners floating proudly in the breeze.

These movements we knew to be indicative of an approaching battle and we rode rapidly to camp to be in readiness to respond promptly to "marching orders." To our surprise they did not come that day, for Hooker's movements had not as yet been sufficiently developed to enable Gen. Lee to form an exact idea of his intentions. The Yankee General kept his troops constantly on the move during the day, marching up and down the River in heavy columns, but the Confederate Commander was watchful and wary, and, as the sequel proved, was not deceived or misled by the strategic evolutions of his adversary. Though the Army of Northern Virginia had been greatly reduced in numbers by the absence of [James] Longstreet[11] and two of his Divisions, the general impression among

---

Louisiana. Another hard-drinking Louisiana officer, Stafford was sometimes overbearing, but also brave to the point of rashness. Warner, *Generals in Gray*, 287; Jones, *Lee's Tigers*, 179.

11. Lieutenant General James Longstreet commanded Lee's I Corps, which was on duty at Suffolk, Virginia, during the spring of 1863. He was the senior lieutenant general in the Confederate army and served Lee well. Warner, *Generals in Gray*, 192–93.

the officers and men was that it still [was] strong enough to cope with Hooker's boasted "finest army on the planet."

April 29th. Before daylight we were awakened by Major Sam Hale, of Maj. General Early's[12] Staff, who brought orders to form the Brigade immediately and prepare to meet the enemy who were reported crossing the River in front of our position to the left of Hamilton's Crossing and just below the "Pratt House."[13] There were no pickets from our Brigade on the River, one of our regiments having been relieved the night before by a Georgia regt.

When the Brigade had been formed and I was sitting on my horse at the head of the column, an affecting incident occurred of which I was the subject. An Irish woman rushed out of her hut in the camp of the 6th Regt., in demi-toilette, with her red shock of hair unkempt and disordered, and coming up to me, raised her long, bony arms to Heaven and fervently called upon the Almighty to cover me with His shield in the day of battle and preserve me from the hands of the enemy. Though the woman was hideously ugly, there was an earnestness and solemnity in her manners that produced a profound impression on the minds of all who saw and heard her. She was a laundress in my Father's Regt. & revered his memory—hence her blessing upon me.

We marched without delay and took position on the [Richmond], Fredericksburg [and Potomac] Railroad, in front and to the left of the Crossing—being the first Brigade to get into line. The 6th Regt. was ordered to the River to relieve a Georgia Regt. that reported their ammunition exhausted. It marched up to the position under a galling fire from the hills on the other side of the River and took their places in the rifle pits. The noble fellows strove manfully

12. Major General Jubal A. Early commanded the division in Jackson's II Corps in which Hays's brigade belonged. The forty-six-year-old officer, a native Virginian, had fought well as a brigade commander at First Manassas and Antietam. As division commander he often clashed with Hays over the Tigers' lawless activity, but he highly respected their fighting ability. One Louisiana officer characterized Early as very witty but noted also that he was irritable and a voracious swearer. *Ibid.,* 79; Jones, *Lee's Tigers,* 143, 177–78; David F. Boyd, "Reminiscences of the War," New Orleans *Times Democrat,* February 7, 1897, in David F. Boyd Scrapbook, Louisiana State University, Baton Rouge.

13. The Pratt House is also known as Smithfield Plantation and is located three and a half miles downstream from Fredericksburg, near Hamilton's Crossing. It is now used as the clubhouse for a local country club. Edward J. Stackpole, *Chancellorsville: Lee's Greatest Victory* (Harrisburg, 1958), 309; *The Official Atlas of the Civil War* (New York, 1958), 31; interview with Doyle Harrison, historian of Fredericksburg and Spotsylvania National Military Park, August 5, 1987, Fredericksburg, Virginia.

to hold their position and keep the enemy from effecting a crossing, and caused many a Yankee to bite the dust by their cool and well directed fire; but the enemy having crossed by means of pontoons and boats above them, the Regt. was flanked and had to seek safety in flight. They fell back, with a loss of 89 men, to the Fredericksburg and Port Royal turnpike, a sunken road equidistant from the River & our fortifications, where they reformed and awaited the further advance of the enemy.

The Yankees soon established two pontoon bridges & continued to pour over the River all day under cover of the high banks that protected them from our fire. In the evening the 6th La. Regt. was relieved by the 19th Ga. About 8 o'clock in the morning of this day and immediately after our picket line had been driven from the River, General "Stonewall" Jackson[14] rode in front of our Brigade, amid the loud cheers of our men, and proceeded to the road along which our advanced regiments (the 5th & 6th) were stationed; from that point he cooly reconnoitred the position of the enemy and exhorted our men to hold the road at all hazards. Though the picket firing was very brisk at the time and the balls fell thick and fast around him, he providentially escaped unhurt, much to our relief who were fearfully looking to see him fall from his horse every moment. After leisualy surveying the enemy from this dangerous post of observation, he shut up his glasses and slowly rode back to the main line. On this occasion Gen. Jackson was clad in a spair new uniform and his unusually spruce appearance excited much attention and remark among his admiring "foot-cavalry," as the soldiers of the 2d Corps were called. Previously, in camp, on the march & in battle, the General had worn an old rusty, sunburnt grey coat and a faded blue cap of a peculiar pattern, the top of which fell forward over his eyes. Alas! a few days afterwards this new uniform served as his burial dress.

April 30th. During the morning nothing of interest occurred along

14. The famous Thomas J. "Stonewall" Jackson commanded Lee's II Corps, to which Hays's brigade was attached. A West Point graduate, Mexican War veteran, and former Virginia Military Institute professor, Jackson was one of Lee's most trusted lieutenants. Although Hays's men now worshiped Jackson, that had not always been the case. Jackson was so well known for being eccentric that Richard Taylor tried unsuccessfully to prevent the 1st Louisiana Brigade from being assigned to his command in 1862. Jackson, in turn, initially distrusted the Tigers because of their frivolity but now, after many hard-fought battles, had formed a close bond with them. Warner, *Generals in Gray*, 151–52; Jones, *Lee's Tigers*, 69–71.

our portion of the line. The enemy on our side of the River were working like beavers on their fortifications; while on the opposite side heavy columns were marching & countermarching, evidently with the intention of deceiving us as to their designs. About fifty yrds. in the rear of the right of our Brigade was a little hill called "Jackson's Hill," because old Stonewall made it his Head Quarters during the first battle of Fredericksburg. This afforded a good position from which to watch the movements of the enemy and there during most of the day were to be seen Generals Lee, Jackson, A. P. Hill[15] and others of lesser note.

A battery of four 20 pounders was in position on this hill and at 5½ o'clock P.M. it opened upon the enemy's lines; the firing seemed to be effective and great commotion was observed among the blue-coats about the "Pratt House." Several Yankee batteries on the other side of the River responded promptly & vigoressly and an artillery duel at long [range] was kept up till dark. The shells burst above and around our Brigade, but did very little execution, wounding only two men of the 9th Regt.; three men of the same regiment were severely wounded by the premature explosion of shells from our own battery.

May 1st. All quiet along our portion of the line—both sides busily engaged in strengthening their fortifications & placing batteries in position. About 10 o'clock a.m., Gen. Lee penetrated the designs of Hooker, it being then very evident that he was sending the larger portion of his army up the River in the direction of Bank's & the United States Fords, leaving one corps (Sedgwick's) to confront our lines about Fredericksburg. A. P. Hill's Corps and two Divisions of Jackson's Corps[16] were immediately dispatched to the vicinity of Chancellorsville, twelve miles distant. Early's Division & Barksdale's Brigade were left to defend the line from Taylor's Hill to Hamilton's Crossing, three and a half miles in length.

15. Major General Ambrose Powell Hill commanded the "Light Division" in Jackson's Corps. The following month he was promoted to lieutenant general and given command of Lee's III Corps. He was killed on April 2, 1865, near Petersburg, Virginia. Warner, *Generals in Gray,* 134–35.

16. Seymour is mistaken. Hill's III Corps was not created until after the Battle of Chancellorsville. To meet Hooker, Lee initially sent Richard Anderson's Division, then Lafayette McLaws'. After leaving Early at Fredericksburg, Jackson quickly put the rest of his corps in motion to follow them. Shelby Foote, *The Civil War: A Narrative* (3 vols.; New York, 1958–74), II, 274–75.

May 2nd. At 1 o'clock P.M. three Brigades of our Division ([John B.] Gordon's, [Robert F.] Hoke's & [William] Smith's) marched out of the breastwork in the direction of Spotsylvania Court House, leaving Hays' & Barksdale's Brigades to hold the enemy in check until nightfall, when they were to follow in the same direction. The design of Gen. Lee evidently was to concentrate his whole army in the vicinity of Chancellorsville, whip Hooker and then turn upon Sedgwick and cut his force into pieces. The 6th & 9th Regts. were sent out to the Hills in the rear of Fredericksburg to reinforce Barksdale and the 5th, 7th & 8th remained in front of the Crossing, being supported by [John B.] Richardson's battery of the Washington Artillery.[17] At 5 o'clock P.M. two large Yankee Brigades advanced against the 7th Regt. and brisk skirmishing took place, lasting until dark; the gallant Seventh holding it's ground manfully, until being flanked on both sides. Col. [Davidson] Penn[18] withdrew it in admirable order, with a loss of one officer and seven men wounded.

Soon after dark these Regts. took up the line of march to join Early; having gone two miles we met the Division returning, the enemy having been discovered to be in heavier force in our front than had been supposed when the movement was commenced by Gen. Early.[19] At 12 o'clock that night the Division resumed it's old position on the railroad, sending skirmishers to the front, who found, much to our surprise, that the Yankees had gone back to the River. From some unaccountable oversight, the enemy had ne-

17. The Washington Artillery was an elite unit of New Orleans volunteers. Organized in 1838, it saw service in the Mexican War and sent four companies to the Army of Northern Virginia in 1861. It was considered one of the best Confederate artillery units and later served in the Spanish-American War and both world wars. Faust, *Encyclopedia of the Civil War,* 806; Booth, comp., *Records of Louisiana Confederate Soldiers,* Vol. III, Pt. II, 311.

18. Colonel Davidson Penn was a native of Lynchburg, Virginia, and a graduate of the Virginia Military Institute. He was also a boyhood friend of Jubal Early, which often placed him in a precarious position in light of the frequent feuds between Early and Hays. Clipping from New Orleans *Times-Picayune,* n.d., in Reminiscences Division, Confederate Veteran Papers; William Harper Forman, Jr., "William P. Harper in War and Reconstruction," *Louisiana History,* XIII (1972), 60.

19. Lee ordered Early to join the rest of the army at Chancellorsville only if Sedgwick left Fredericksburg, but these orders were misunderstood and Early's three brigades left prematurely. The mistake was soon corrected, and Early returned to his original position. *The War of the Rebellion: A Compilation of the Official Records of the Union and Confederate Armies* (130 vols.; Washington, D.C., 1880–1901), Ser. I, Vol. XXV, Pt. I, 800–802 (hereinafter cited as *OR*).

glected to take advantage of our absence to strike the Railroad at Hamilton's Crossing; thence he could have marched to Guinea Station & cut our railroad communication with Richmond. During this day very heavy artillery firing was heard in the direction of Chancellorsville, where a great battle was raging.[20]

May 3d. At 7 o'clock a.m., the Brigade marched under a furious cannonade to a point above Fredericksburg opposite the little town of Falmouth, nearly four miles distant, where we arrived just in time to prevent the enemy from turning the left of Barksdale's Brigade & taking possession of some commanding heights, which would have compelled our whole line to fall back from it's entrenchments. Had the Yankees succeeded in this movement, Gen. Early's Division would have been cut off from the main army. Two hour's after we took our new position (on Barksdale's left), Gen. Sedgwick, after having made three ineffectual efforts to capture Marye's Heights—losing thereby at least one thousand men[21]—succeeded in taking that stronghold away from the men who had so gallantly defended it, Barksdale's Mississippians.

Here I will mention an incident connected with this affair that is forcibly illustrative of Yankee cunning and duplicity. Half an hour before the storming of the Heights, Sedgwick sent a flag of truce to a Colonel commanding the forces at that point, requesting permission to attend to the wants of the wounded Yankees that were lying in front of our line. The unsuspecting Mississippian inexcusably permitted the flag of truce party to come within a few feet of his line. The bearer of the flag was, as we were subsequently informed, an officer of high rank in the disguise of a subaltern—a shrewd, Keen, observant fellow who made his eyes do their full duty during the interview. He quickly perceived how weak & extended our line was and that a very important ravine between Taylor's & Marye's Heights was entirely undefended. Twenty minutes after the return of the flag the enemy, who had almost his entire force in the streets of Fredericksburg, rushed up the ravine and made a dash at the Heights, which he soon captured—taking between two and three

20. At Chancellorsville, Lee and Hooker were engaged in a slugfest. Late on May 2, Jackson launched a brilliant flank attack that nearly rolled up the Yankee line. Faust, *Encyclopedia of the Civil War,* 126.

21. Sedgwick lost approximately 1,500 men. Foote, *Civil War,* II, 126.

hundred of Barksdale's men, six guns and thirty-five officers and men of the Washington Artillery. The artillerists fought with great bravery and determination and did not yield until they had been entirely surrounded, several of them being bayonetted at the guns. One of our Regts., the 6th, which had been left to support the batteries on Lee's Hill, came very near being surrounded and captured, and escaped with a loss of twenty-seven men killed and wounded.

The capture of Marye's Heights necessitated the falling back of our Division to a point on the "Telegraph Road," two miles distant from Fredericksburg. Notwithstanding the numerical superiority of the enemy's forces—he having 30,000 opposed to our 8,000 men—he did not attempt to pursue us. In the charge upon the Heights the Yankees were generously drunk; Sedgwick always plied his troops with whiskey when he wanted them to charge.[22] All day long the firing of artillery in the direction of Chancellorsville was very heavy.

May 4th. At 6 o'clock a.m. Gordon's Georgia Brigade charged and easily retook Marye's Heights. Our Brigade & Hoke's marched towards the "Plank Road." After proceeding three miles in that direction we were ordered to take position in front of the enemy posted at and around the "Darmon House,"[23] which we did at 10½ o'clock; Hoke's Brigade occupying the front line and we supporting it. The left wing of Sedgwick extended about three quarters of a mile beyond our extreme right and Gen. Lee being informed that the odds against us were too heavy, sent the Divisions of [Lafayette] McLaws and [Richard] Anderson to our support. Our Division connected with Anderson's right and at 4 o'clock P.M. Hays' Brigade was placed opposite to the extreme left of the enemy. It was the intention of Gen. Lee to order a general advance at 2 o'clock P.M. but the attack was delayed by the tardy arrival of McLaws & Anderson, who had been fighting the evening before at Chancellorsville.

At 5½ o'clock the whole line advanced and the charge of Hays' Brigade was pronounced by General officers—among them Gen.

22. Charges of drunkenness on the part of the enemy was a common accusation used by both sides during the Civil War. There is no evidence to support Seymour's claims about Sedgwick's men.
23. Seymour is referring to the Downman House, two and a half miles east of Salem Church, which served as Lee's headquarters on May 4, 1863. Interview with Harrison, August 5, 1987, in Fredericksburg, Virginia.

Lee himself, who witnessed it from Taylor's Hill—to have been one of the most dashing and brilliant of the war.[24] At the order to charge our gallant fellows rushed up the high range of Hills in their front under a heavy fire and across a broad plain raked by the heavy 20 & 30 pounder batteries on Stafford Heights. Four field batteries & three lines of infantry were in our front; so impetuous was this charge that two of these lines were broken & driven for some distance, while the artillery was forced from the field. As we were approaching the third line, night coming on & the woods the woods [sic] dark, Hoke's North Carolina Brigade, which had come in behind us, mistook us for Yankees and opened a galling fire upon our rear, while the enemy engaged us in front. This untoward accident forced us to abandon the attack & march by the left flank out of our critical position.[25]

During this movement many of our officers and men lost their way in the woods and were taken prisoners; among the former were Col. Stafford & Major [Henry L. N.] Williams[26] of the 9th Regt.; Lt. Col. [Trevanion D.] Lewis[27] & Major [Alcibiades] DeBlanc[28] of the 8th; Lt. Col. [Thomas M.] Terry[29] of the 7th, & Capt. [Thomas H.] Biscoe[30] of the 5th. Had this attack been made two hours earlier, Sedgwick would have been cut off from the United States Ford, his only route of escape, and the whole of his corps

24. Both Early and Lee watched the attack from atop Taylor's Hill. When it appeared that Hays would succeed, Early jubilantly threw his hat on the ground shouting, "Those damned Louisiana fellows may steal as much as they please now!" Lee then slapped his hands together and muttered, "Thank God! the day is ours." This joy turned to dismay, however, when the attack broke up against the last Union position. Clipping from New Orleans *Times Democrat*, n.d., in Reminiscences Division, Confederate Veteran Papers.

25. This accident certainly contributed to the attack's failure, but it would be more accurate to attribute the assault's collapse to a combination of fatigue, disorganization, and stubborn resistance from the third Union line. Jones, *Lee's Tigers*, 154.

26. Henry L. N. Williams was mortally wounded at Gettysburg. Booth, comp., *Records of Louisiana Confederate Soldiers*, Vol. III, Pt. II, 1095–96.

27. Trevanion D. Lewis was wounded at Antietam and later killed at Gettysburg. On his military record was written: "He was an excellent officer and very much regretted by his Regiment. A gallant, brave and military man." *Ibid.*, Pt. I, 753.

28. Alcibiades DeBlanc was actually a lieutenant colonel, having been promoted on April 3, 1863. A few months later he was promoted to colonel after being wounded at Gettysburg. Written on his military record: "A perfect gentleman and excellent officer. All respected, obeyed and loved him." He retired in August, 1864. *Ibid.*, II, 572–73.

29. Lieutenant Colonel Thomas M. Terry, from St. Tammany Parish, was only twenty-five years old. *Ibid.*, Vol. III, Pt. II, 793.

30. Twenty-four-year-old Thomas H. Bisco was wounded earlier during a skirmish and would be killed the following year in the Wilderness. *Ibid.*, I, 194.

captured; but the delay was unavoidable, owing to the distance our re-enforcements—wearied out by fighting all the previous day—had to traverse.

That night the whole Yankee army recrossed the River and the great battle of Chancellorsville, or Second Fredericksburg, had been fought and won. The loss of our Brigade on this day was as follows: Killed, 73; wounded, 295; missing (prisoners), 293. Total, 661.[31] The Brigade went into action with about 1,500 men. A great portion of our loss was caused by the raking fire of the enemy's big guns on Stafford's Heights; at one time a large shell fell into the ranks of the 9th Regt., with which I went into the fight, and exploding, Killed & wounded *seventeen men*. We remained on the field in line of battle until 2 o'clock a.m.

May 5th. Before daylight the Brigade occupied the trenches in front of Lee's Hill; but when day broke we found that the enemy had gone, leaving in our immediate front two Napoleon guns[32] which in their haste they had abandoned. At 9 o'clock a.m., we marched in the direction of the Plank Road, being treated on the way to an occasional shell from the Yankee guns on the other side of the River; before reaching there we were ordered back to Hamilton's Crossing, where we arrived at 5 o'clock in the evening. The rain soon began to descend in torrents and continued to do so all night and the following day, occasioning great inconvinience to our men who were almost entirely without shelter.

May 6th. Brigade in same position—nothing noteworthy occurring.

May 7th. At 10 o'clock a.m. reoccupied our old camp, one mile from the Crossing, from which we marched on the 29th ult. Here we remained until the 5th of June, nothing transpiring to break the usual monotony of camp life.

On the 28th of May I received the appointment (unsolicited by me) of Assistant Adjutant General in the Confederate States Army; my commission being signed by James A. Seddon, Secretary of War and bearing [the] date May 26th, 1863. My rank was that of

31. Official returns give Hays's losses for the entire campaign at 369 dead and wounded and approximately 300 captured. *OR*, Vol. XXV, Pt. I, 808; Richmond *News*, May 19, 1863, in Civil War Scrapbook, 1862–64, Tulane University, New Orleans, Louisiana.

32. The Napoleon was a commonly used twelve-pound smoothbore artillery piece. Faust, *Encyclopedia of the Civil War*, 520.

Captain and I was assigned to duty with Brig. Gen. Harry T. Hays, Comdg. 1st La. Brigade, Army of Northern Virginia.

The Battle of Chancellorsville resulted in a great and glorious victory to the Confederate arms; the boasting Yankee commander, "Fighting Joe Hooker," as he had been dubbed by his bragging admirers and followers, had been very neatly and effectively thwarted in his proposed "On to Richmond" excursion, and his "finest Army on the planet" had been badly whipped by a force not one-half of its strength. While we naturally indulged in considerable elation of spirits at the achievement of this great victory, our hearts were shrouded in the deepest grief at the loss of our beloved Corps Commander, the incomparable Jackson. He was shot at night by a party of Mahone's Virginia Brigade, who mistook him for a Federal officer. Never have I witnessed a more profound, heartfelt & universal sorrow as pervaded the whole army on this occasion.[33]

33. While on a reconnaissance beyond his lines on the night of May 2, Jackson was mistakenly shot by members of the 18th North Carolina, James H. Lane's Brigade (not William Mahone's unit). His left arm was amputated, and he died from complications on May 10. Foote, Civil War, II, 301–302, 319; Burke Davis, They Called Him Stonewall: A Life of Lt. General T. J. Jackson, C.S.A. (New York, 1954), 425.

THE CAMPAIGN IN
PENNSYLVANIA

THE Confederate victory at Chancellorsville had been stunning, but it came at a high price. The loss of Jackson and heavy casualties among other officers forced Lee to reorganize his army before initiating any new maneuvers. A new III Corps was formed and placed under A. P. Hill, while Richard S. Ewell was promoted to lieutenant general and given command of Jackson's II Corps. Ewell, a West Point graduate and veteran of the Mexican War, had commanded a crack division under Jackson for over a year. Known as an eccentric, the bald-headed Ewell had lost a leg at Groveton in August, 1862. While he recovered from the wound, Ewell's division was temporarily taken over by Early during the Fredericksburg and Chancellorsville campaigns. But now Ewell had recuperated, and the members of Hays's brigade were happy to see their old commander rewarded with the command of the corps. The irascible Early was then promoted to permanent division commander.[1]

May, 1863, was a time for decisions to be made by the Confederate high command. Pressure was on Lee to help alleviate the critical situation at Vicksburg, currently under attack by federal forces. Lee resisted efforts to detach part of his army to reinforce Vicksburg, opting instead for a second invasion of the North. A thrust into Pennsylvania, Lee claimed, would draw Yankee forces away from the beleaguered Mississippi city, garnish badly needed supplies for his men, keep the enemy off balance in Virginia, and strengthen the Northern peace movement. Accordingly, in early June the Army of Northern Virginia struck out northward. For Seymour and his comrades it was a glorious time. Sensing that they were about to experience a historic moment, the victorious rebels moved confidently and proudly toward Pennsylvania and the sleepy town of Gettysburg.[2]

---

1. Warner, *Generals in Gray*, 84–85; Jones, *Lee's Tigers*, 156.
2. Faust, *Encyclopedia of the Civil War*, 307–308.

GEN. Lee having fought two battles on the line of the Rappahannock with no other results than driving the Federals back to their strong & unassailable position on the hills of Stafford [Heights], resolved to maneuver Hooker out of Virginia and to transfer hostilities to the enemy's territory. Such a movement, if successful, would break up the Yankee plans for the ensuing campaign, relieve threatened points in other portions of the Confederacy, and satisfy the clamor that pervaded the South for an invasion of the North to make the Yankees feel more sensibly the disastrous effects of the war they had inaugurated. The Army commenced to move on the 3d of June, when McLaws' Division marched in the direction of Culpepper Court House. The Army of Northern Virginia had been divided into three *corps d'armee:* Lieut. General Longstreet commanding the 1st; Lieut. Gen. Ewell the 2d; and Lieut. Gen. A. P. Hill the 3d.

June 5th. Broke camp at midnight, o[u]r pickets on the River having been relieved by [Ambrose Ransom] Wright's Georgia Brigade, Hill's Corps. Marched in a North Western direction over a very rugged country. At daylight the Yankee balloon was discried and the aeronaut must have discovered that our troops were on the march; however, the display of force by Hill's corps at Fredericksburg must have blinded the enemy as to the extent of the movement. Marched this day *22 miles.*

June 6th. Resumed the march at sunrise, halting at 10 o'clock A.M. near Locust Grove, Orange Co[unty], where we remained all day awaiting the developement of the enemy's intention; he having crossed a force below Fredericksburg near the "Bernard House"[3] & opposite the position that our Brigade had left, with the apparent intention of once more moving against our lines stretching from Fredericksburg to Hamilton's Crossing. Distance marched *8 miles.*

June 7th. Had a hard days march, passing in sight of Slaughter Mountain, where Gen. Jackson in August last won a victory over Gen. [John] Pope.[4] Camped at night within two miles of Culpepper C[ourt] H[ouse]. Distance marched, *20 miles.*

3. The Bernard House was a plantation on the south bank of the Rappahannock River about a mile downstream from Fredericksburg. Edward J. Stackpole, *Drama on the Rappahannock: The Fredericksburg Campaign* (Harrisburg, 1957), 162, 177.

4. The Battle of Slaughter Mountain, or Cedar Mountain, occurred at the beginning of the Second Manassas Campaign on August 9, 1862. Although poorly fought by Jackson, the

June 8th. Started at daylight, passed through Culpepper C[ourt] H[ouse] and camped two miles beyond the town. Longstreet & Ewell's Corps were now in the vicinity of that place, while [J. E. B.] Stuart's[5] Cavalry Corps were concentrated near Brandy Station. Distance marched, *4 miles*.

June 9th. On this day a large force of the enemy's cavalry, strongly supported by infantry, crossed the Rappahannock at Beverly's & Kelley's Fords and attacked Gen. Stuart. A very severe engagement ensued, continuing from early in the morning until late in the afternoon, when the enemy were forced to recross the River with heavy loss, leaving four hundred prisoners, three pieces of artillery and several stands of colors in our hands. This was one of the most stubborn and bloody cavalry fights of the War, and both sides lost heavily. By this movement Hooker sought to drive Stuart back from Brandy Station in order to develope our infantry force at & around Culpepper. At 2 o'clock in the afternoon Early's Division, our Brigade included, was marched to the support of Stuart; but our services were not needed and we bivouacked that night on the battle field.[6] Distance marched this day, 7 miles.

June 10th. The enemy having disappeared from our front, we retraced our steps to our old camp north of Culpepper. At 4 P.M. [we] started our march, after a long and vexatious delay, and camped at night at Hazel Run. Distance, *16 miles*.

June 11th. Left camp at 5½ a.m.—passed through Sperryville and went into camp early in the afternoon. Distance, *20 miles*.

June 12. Marched at daylight—crossed the Blue Ridge [Mountains] at Chester Gap, going through to Front Royal to the Shenandoah River. Distance, *23 miles*.

June 13th. Forded the Shenandoah at 3½ o'clock A.M. taking the

---

battle was a victory over the Union Army of Virginia. Faust, *Encyclopedia of the Civil War*, 121–22.

5. James Ewell Brown Stuart, Lee's flamboyant cavalry commander, was one of the most famous Confederate generals. In June, 1863, he was a major general and commanded all the cavalry in the Army of Northern Virginia. Warner, *Generals in Gray*, 296–97.

6. To gather intelligence about the Confederate movement, Hooker sent Major General Alfred Pleasonton and 11,000 troopers across the Rappahannock on June 9. The resulting clash at Brandy Station was the largest cavalry battle of the war. Although Stuart finally forced the Yankees back, it was a difficult fight for him and marked the end of the Confederate cavalry's domination over its Union counterpart. Stuart lost 253 men in the battle and Pleasonton 936. Faust, *Encyclopedia of the Civil War*, 76; Emory M. Thomas, *Bold Dragoon: The Life of J. E. B. Stuart* (New York, 1986), 219–31.

Winchester turnpike & passed by the grave of Major Aaron Davis, formerly Commissary of our Brigade, who was killed in the battle of Front Royal last year.[7] At 7 o'clock we diverged from the main road, taking the one to Newtown; marching through that place, we halted at 11½ o'clock within three miles of Winchester. At that place Gen. [Robert] Milroy had from ten to twelve thousand Yankees behind very strong fortifications[8] and had sent word to Gen. Ewell that he intended defending the town until (to use his classical language) "Hell froze over." The sequel will show that he did not tarry there long enough to learn whether any such extraordinary signs of frigidity had been observed in the infernal regions. We formed line of battle on the left of the 'pike, near Barton's Mill & in the rear of Kernstown, the scene of the first important engagement fought by Jackson in the Valley of the Shenandoah.[9] The Yankees were in strong force in our front and skirmishing briskly with the cavalry of Gen. [Albert Gallatin] Jenkins. About 4 o'clock P.M. Gordon's & Hays' Brigades advanced and drove the enemy to their entrenchments near the town. We remained in line of battle all night. Distance marched this day, *17 miles.*

In front of Winchester Gen. Ewell had two Divisions, Early's and [Edward] Johnson's;[10] Gen. [Robert] Rodes[11] had been detached from the corps and sent to Berryville with instructions to dislodge the Yankees posted there and cut off communication between Winchester and the Potomac. On the approach of Rodes the force at Berryville retreated upon Winchester.

June 14. Gen. Ewell, at the suggestion of Gen. Early, determined to take Winchester by a flank movement rather than by a general

7. Davis was killed on May 23, 1862, at the Battle of Front Royal while leading a pursuit against fleeing Union soldiers. Jones, *Lee's Tigers,* 74–75.

8. Major General Robert Milroy actually had six to eight thousand men at Winchester. Warner, *Generals in Blue,* 326.

9. Under orders to tie down the Union forces in the Shenandoah Valley, Jackson attacked the federals at Kernstown on March 23, 1862. But he mishandled the battle and was repulsed, losing several hundred men. Faust, *Encyclopedia of the Civil War,* 415.

10. Major General Edward Johnson, a Virginian, commanded Jackson's old division in the II Corps. The 2nd Louisiana Brigade, consisting of the 1st, 2nd, 10th, 14th, and 15th Louisiana Volunteers, was in his command. Warner, *Generals in Gray,* 158–59; Jones, *Lee's Tigers,* 156.

11. Major General Robert Rodes commanded D. H. Hill's old division and had won laurels and a promotion for his role in leading Jackson's flank attack against Hooker at Chancellorsville. He was mortally wounded at Winchester, Virginia, on September 19, 1864. Warner, *Generals in Gray,* 263.

assault. To carry out this plan, all the Brigades of our Division—except Gordon's, which remained to make a demonstration in front to engage the attention of the enemy and [Lt. Col. H. P.] Jones's battalion of artillery—were led by Gen. Early by a blind and circuitous road leading to a thickly wooded hill west of the town between the Romney and Pughtown roads. On the left of Winchester are a series of hills rising higher & higher as they extend towards the West; those near the town were crowned with strong and elaborately made redoubts, the most prominent of which was the "Flag Staff Fort." Four hundred yards to the West of this Fort, and commanding it, was a redoubt of six guns, and this was the one that we were to assault. Once in our possession, we could soon silence the remaining works and force Milroy to evacuate Winchester or surrender his army. So si[l]ently was the march performed that we did not encounter on the way a picket or scout of the enemy.

At 6 o'clock P.M. our artillery opened a rapid and well directed fire upon the redoubt, some of the shells explode over the work while others struck the parapet, tearing great holes in it and sending the dirt high up in the air. So taken by surprise were the Yankees that they made no response for several minutes, when, recovering themselves, they replied with considerable spirit. Our Brigade was formed in a thick woods that skirted the Hill, with the 6th, 7th and 9th Regts. in the first line and the 5th & 8th in the second. Arriving at the foot of the Hill, still under cover of the woods, Gen. Hays sent me to Gen. Early to let him know that we were ready for the assault. Gen. Early told me to instruct Gen. Hays to wait for orders—that he wished to dismount some of the enemy's guns before the attack by infantry commenced. Gen. Hays, supposing by the changed direction of the enemy's fire that they had discovered his position and thinking that the favorable moment had arrived, took the responsibility of ordering his Brigade forward; the result proved him to have acted wisely.

Emerging from the woods, our boys had to cross several open fields, jump fences, etc., but so hot was the fire of our artillery that the Yankee infantry had to Keep so close behind their breastworks that they did not observe us until we had reached an abattis of felled timber some 150 yards from the redoubt. While scrambling through this, our artillery ceased firing and the Yankee infantry opened a brisk fire upon us; but so impetuous was the charge of our men that in a few minutes they were over the breastworks, driving the enemy out in great haste and confusion. The Yankee artillerymen, who were regulars, strove hard to save their guns, but by shooting the horses we prevented them from taking away a single piece or caisson. In this charge we captured six of the finest rifled guns, but took very few prisoners, the Yanks being too nimble of foot for us. Our loss was 79 in Killed & wounded—far less than we had anticipated.

After our men had effected an entrance into the redoubt, Adjutant John Orr[12] of the Sixth Regiment, seeing a Yankee color-bearer with a guard of two men carrying off his flag, ran after him to secure it; overtaking them, Orr seized the standard and with his sword single-handed commenced a fight with the three guardians, and after a short contest he was run through the body with a bayonet and the flag carried away. Strange to say, Orr recovered from his wound. Capt. [Charles A.] Thompson, commanding the Louisiana Guard Battery[13]—a gallant officer and an estimable gentleman— was wounded by a shell, from the effects of which he died that night. His wound was in the wrist & comparatively slight, but he would not leave his guns in time to have it properly attended to and consequently died from loss of blood.

Soon after the redoubt had been taken, the enemy were seen massing in the valley beyond, apparently with the intention of attempting it's recapture; a party of volunteer cannoneers from the 5th & 6th Regts. turned the captured guns and by a few well directed shots drove them away. Shortly after, Jones' Artillery came up to our new position and opened upon the "Star Fort," which promptly replied; shot and shell fell thick and fast about us, but did very little execution. We remained all night at the redoubt.

June 15th. At dawn we discovered that the enemy had evacuated Winchester; they were forced to this by the capture by Hays' Brigade of the redoubt, which rendered all the other works untenable. Milroy retreated in the direction of Martinsburg; but Gen. Ewell

12. John Orr was the twenty-three-year-old adjutant for Hays's brigade. He had been wounded at Antietam and was later captured at Rappahannock Station on November 7, 1863. Booth, comp., *Records of Louisiana Confederate Soldiers,* Vol. III, Book II, 44.

13. The Louisiana Guard Battery was organized in August, 1861, under Captain Camille E. Girardey and for a while was a part of Hays's brigade. Dimitry, *Louisiana,* 322e.

had dispatched Johnson's Division by a circuitous route to intercept him and two thirds of the Yankee Army were taken prisoners, though Milroy escaped with a small escort of cavalry. The fruits of our victory were: 4,500 prisoners; twenty-nine pieces of artillery; 280 waggons, and a vast amount of military stores.[14] It is universally conceeded that the capture of Winchester was mainly due to the action of Hays' Brigade and Gen. Ewell told me that he would give orders that the range of Hills West of the town should be called on the field maps "Louisiana Ridge." The people of Winchester, who had suffered terribly from the tyrannical acts of the infamous Milroy, hailed his discomfiture with the most raptuous expressions of delight.

On this day Gen. Rodes captured Martinsburg, taking seven hundred prisoners, five pieces of artillery, and a considerable quantity of stores.[15] These operations cleared the Valley of Federal troops, the garrison retiring from Harper's Ferry to Maryland Heights.[16] Distance marched *7 miles;* we went into camp out on the Martinsburg road, within sight of the place where my Dear Father had encamped the year before. Called on Gen. Ewell to give him a list of the casualties in our Brigade; the old Gen. was very profuse in his praise of the action of our Brigade. Also called on Gen. Early, whose Head Quarters were in Winchester; tickled him by repeating what a Yankee Colonel (a prisoner) had said about his flanking Milroy. The "Fed" declared that the "Johnny Rebs" had lied in reporting that "Stonewall Jackson" was dead—that there was no officer in either army that could have executed that movement but "Old Jack."

June 16th. In camp all day.

June 17th. Broke camp at 2 P.M. and marched to within six miles of Charlestown; a dull, uneventful day. Distance, *18 miles.*

June 18th. Started at daylight & went into camp early in the after-

14. Milroy's losses were put at 95 dead, 348 wounded, almost 4,000 prisoners, 23 cannons, and 300 wagons. Ewell lost 47 dead, 219 wounded, and 3 missing. Faust, *Encyclopedia of the Civil War,* 835; OR, Vol. XXVII, Pt. II, 439–42.

15. Actually, Rodes's victory occurred on June 14. He was advancing toward Maryland through Berryville and Martinsburg when he cleared the latter town of Yankees. OR, Vol. XXVII, Pt. II, 548–50.

16. Maryland Heights is a high ridge on the north bank of the Potomac River that dominates Harpers Ferry. Espisito, ed., *West Point Atlas,* 66.

noon within four miles of Shepherdstown—a place called after Rezin D[avis] Shepherd[17] of New Orleans; who formerly resided there. Took tea at the house of a Mr. Schley,[18] a nephew of Ex. Gov. [William] Schley of Georgia, whom my grandfather, years ago, wounded in a duel.[19] Remained in this camp until the 23d inst. Distance marched, *18 miles*.

June 23d. On the move at daylight, passed through Shepherdstown & forded the Potomac. The [water] was very high and it was amusing to see the long lines of naked men fording it—their clothing and accountrements slung to their guns and carried above their heads to keep them dry. The water was very cold and the men as they entered it would scream and shout most boisterously. We passed through Sharpsburg & over the battle field[20]—through Boonsboro and Waynesboro, & camped near the last named town. In Waynesboro the people are strongly "Union" in their proclivities, and their countenances and actions did not indicate much joy at our arrival. Our men got quantities of liquor here and I had great trouble in keeping them in ranks. Inspector General [John] New, being taken sick, had to stop on the way and I had to discharge his duties, as well as those of Adjutant Genl. during the remainder of the march to Gettysburg. Distance accomplished, *17 miles*.

June 24th. Moved at 7 o'clock A.M. and stopped at the extensive iron mills of Thadeus Stevens,[21] one of the vilest, most unprincipled

17. Shepherd's father, Thomas, established a fort on the Potomac River about twelve miles above Harpers Ferry in the late 1700s. Rezin was born there in 1784. He later became a prosperous New Orleans businessman but retired at the beginning of the Civil War and moved back to Virginia until the war was over. Rezin D. Shepherd biography, in Biographical File, Louisiana Collection, Tulane University, New Orleans.

18. Seymour apparently stayed in the house known as Rockland, located about three miles south of Shepherdstown. It was owned by John Schley, who, ironically, was a Union sympathizer. Interview with Ben Schley, November 5, 1987, Shepherdstown, West Virginia.

19. William Schley, who had a distinguished career as a judge, legislator, and congressman, was elected Georgia's governor in 1835. Unfortunately, the details of the duel are unknown. Clement A. Evans, *Georgia: Comprising Sketches of Counties, Towns, Events, Institutions and Persons. Arranged in Cyclopedic Form*, ed. Allen D. Candler (3 vols.; Atlanta, 1906), III, 248–49.

20. The Battle of Sharpsburg, or Antietam, took place on September 17, 1862. In a vicious fight, later characterized as the bloodiest day in American history, Union General George B. McClellan halted Lee's invasion into Maryland. Hays's brigade was badly shot up that day, suffering a 60 percent casualty rate in thirty minutes. Faust, *Encyclopedia of the Civil War*, 18–19; Jones, *Lee's Tigers*, 130.

21. Thaddeus Stevens, a Republican congressman from Pennsylvania, was famous for his

& most fanatical of the Yankee Abolition Congressmen. Permission having been granted, our men took pleasure in helping themselves most bountifully to the products of his broad and fertile acres. Distance, *16 miles*.

June 25th. In camp all day, luxuriating on old Thad's provider and good things generally.

June 26th. Left camp at 11 o'clock A.M.—a rainy & most disagreeable day. By orders of Gen. Early, our pioneers set fire to and destroyed the two large iron mills of Stevens, together with the adjoining storehouses. This was the only occasion during the Pennsylvania Campaign when private property was destroyed by our troops[22]—We crossed South Mountain and camped at night near the town of Gettysburg. While preparing to cook rations, news came of a large force of Pennsylvania militia being six miles distant, skirmishing with our cavalry. Two of our regiments were dispatched to attend to them; the militia, who no doubt had previously resolved to die if need be in the defense of their homes and friends, changed their minds when they caught a glimpse of our two little regiments in the distance and most precipitately and ingloriously fled the field. Darkness coming on, our men returned to camp, weary from their long and useless march in the rain and mud. Distance, *15 miles,* with *12 miles* additional for the two regts. that went on the above expedition.

June 27. Resumed the march at daylight. The men having had too free access to liquor, of which there were large quantities in Gettysburg, many of them were drunk and caused me much trouble to make them keep up with the column. Some of the most obstreperous I had put into the cooking utensils waggons, where they had a rough and disagreeable ride on the sharp sides and projecting legs of the pots & kettles, which sobered them speedily. These drunken fellows would not ride far before they begged most pitiously to be

---

radical stand against slavery and the South. As chairman of the powerful Ways and Means Committee, he pushed for black equality and the use of black troops. He was a leading Radical Republican during Reconstruction. Faust, *Encyclopedia of the Civil War,* 718.

22. In his memoirs, Early claimed that he destroyed Stevens' property in retaliation for similar acts of destruction against Southern civilians. Jubal Anderson Early, *War Memoirs: Autobiographical Sketch and Narrative of the War Between the States,* ed. Frank E. Vandiver (1912; rpr. Bloomington, 1960), 255–56.

taken out and allowed to walk.[23] Marched to a point north of Berlin. Distance, *21 miles*.

June 28th. Marched at sun-rise and reached the city of York, Penn., and camped on a high hill two miles from town. The surrounding country was in a high state of cultivation and from our camp presented a beautiful appearance with its immense fields of golden grain that flashed in the sunlight—dotted here and there with neat little cottages and large substantially built barns wh[ich] were literally bursting with wheat, oats & corn. Most of the barns in this section of Pennsylvania are larger and more finely built than the dwellings of the farmers; the Dutch lords of the soil invariably bestow more care and attention on their crops and stock than they do on their families.

During our march the inhabitants were treated with the greatest kindness and consideration, Gen. Lee having issued the most stringent orders against the molestation of their persons or property.[24] Everything that was taken for the use of the army was paid for, except in some cases when the tender of the money was refused. Stragglers would sometimes make predatory excursions into barnyards and dairies belonging to persons who were disposed to be inimical and unaccomodating—this was unavoidable; but I did not hear of a single instance of a citizen being insulted or his property damaged. The forbearance of our troops in this respect showed the admirable discipline they were under; hundreds of them from the far South had had their own houses and farms destroyed or despoiled by the Northern Vandals, and their families turned out

23. Apparently, Hays precipitated Seymour's troubles by issuing a pint ration of whiskey to each man before marching out of Gettysburg. "The whole brigade got drunk," wrote one officer. "I never saw such a set in my life." Straggling and fighting plagued the brigade all day. Joseph Warren Jackson to R. Stark Jackson, July 20, 1863, in David F. Boyd Civil War Papers, Louisiana State University, Baton Rouge; Thomas Benton Reed, *A Private in Gray* (Camden, Ark., 1905), 40–41.

24. In General Order 73, Lee issued explicit orders that private property was to be respected and that all provisions taken be paid for—although with worthless Confederate money. The ragged rebels obediently toed the line. General Ewell wrote his wife, "It is wonderful how well our hungry, foot sore, ragged men behave in this land of plenty—better than at home." A Louisiana officer echoed this sentiment, claiming the Tigers "behave worse in Va. than they did in Penn." Richard S. Ewell to Lizzie Ewell, June 24, 1863, in Richard S. Ewell Papers, Library of Congress; Jackson to Jackson, July 20, 1863, in Boyd Civil War Papers; Douglas Southall Freeman, *R. E. Lee: A Biography* (4 vols.; New York, 1935), III, 56–57.

of doors to starve or live on the charity of their more fortunate neighbors.

The Pennsylvania farmers had sent most of their horses and mules to the other side of the Susquehannah River to prevent their falling into our hands. As our army was in great need of animals for transportation purposes, the Quartermasters were ordered to scour the country in quest of them & to pay for the same in Confederate money. Horses were found in bedrooms, parlours, lofts of barns and other out of the way place[s]. Major [John G.] Campbell, Acting Quartermaster of our Brigade, called at a large, finely furnished house, the owner of which he had learned was possessed of a splendid horse. The proprietor stoutly denied that he had such an animal but, unfortunately for him, a neigh from an adjoining room gave the *nay* to his assertion and revealed the hiding place of the much desired quadruped. The Major quietly opened the door and there in an elegant parlour, comfortably stalled in close proximity to a costly rosewood piano, stood a noble looking horse; though not of the "Ukraine breed," he was one of the best specimens of the Pennsylvania "Connestoga." With some difficulty the Major led his prize forth from the novel stable and paid for him in the current funds of the Confederate realm.

Gen. Gordon, with his Brigade, was sent twelve miles beyond York to take possession of the great bridge that spanned the Susquehannah at that place. On his arrival he found a small force of militia drawn up in battle array to defend it; but a few shots from his artillery put these gallant defenders to flight. As they fled across the bridge they set fire to the costly structure; this communicated to a village near by and would have destroyed it had not the Georgians rushed in and extinguished the flames—a strong contrast to the inhuman conduct of Federal troops on similar occasions during the war. I was told by a distinguished General that, had Gordon succeeded in saving the bridge from destruction, it was Gen. Early's intention to carry his troops across the River, mount them and make a raid through the country; he would destroy railroad communications with Baltimore and Philadelphia and take Harrisburg in reverse while Ewell attacked it in front.[25]

25. In keeping with his general plan to threaten Washington, Baltimore, and Philadelphia, Lee had ordered Ewell to move on to Harrisburg. But Gordon's failure to save the

Distance marched this day, *13 miles*.

June 29. Brigade in camp all day. I visited the town of York in the afternoon; found it quite a pretty place of about twelve thousand inhabitants. Some of the public buildings are exceedingly tasteful and imposing structures. All the stores were closed and I was much disappointed in not being able to purchase articles of clothing of which I stood in great need. Through the kindness of my friend Major Hale, of Gen. Early's Staff, who was acting Provost Marshal, I got into the back door of a very large fancy store, where I purchased a bottle of old Cognac brandy and a few other articles. The proprietor of the establishment was a Baltimore woman, who appeared to be greatly rejoiced at the advent of Confederate troops and declared her willingness to accept Confederate money in exchange for anything contained in her store.

The inhabitants professed to be "Copper-heads"[26] and opposed to the Federal Conscription Act and the further prosecution of the war. Not much faith to be placed in their professions; they are a mean, selfish, sordid people, who would profess or do anything to save their money & property. Soon after we entered the State of Pennsylvania, Gen. Early was waited upon by a deputation of citizens who informed him that there were thousands of men in that part of the State who were opposed to the war & who belonged to a Secret Society called the "Knights of the Golden Circle,"[27] who had their distinctive signs, grips and countersigns; all of which were imparted to the General, who in turn, gave them to his officers.

Much to our surprise, hundreds of people in the towns through which we passed greeted us with these signs and we joyfully accepted them as proofs of the anti-war feeling that pervaded the

---

bridge at Wrightsville upset the plan. Early in particular was disappointed, for he had planned to mount his division on captured horses and launch a massive raid into the Harrisburg area. *OR*, Vol. XXVII, Pt. II, 315–16, 464–68.

26. Copperheads, or Peace Democrats, were Northern Democrats who opposed the war. They believed the Union could not be restored through force, and they particularly opposed President Abraham Lincoln's plan to emancipate the slaves. Supposedly they were called Copperheads because some wore copper pennies to identify themselves as members. Faust, *Encyclopedia of the Civil War,* 564.

27. The Knights of the Golden Circle was founded in the South in 1854. Its original purpose was to annex Mexico as slave territory, but secession soon became its main goal, and new chapters sprang up in the border states. Sworn to secrecy, members engaged in subversive activities in Union territory during the Civil War. *Ibid.,* 420.

country. When we reached York we found that these professions and demonstrations were hollow and hypocritical. Just in advance of our army two Yankees from one of the New England States travelled through the country, professing to be high officers of a New York lodge of the "Knights of the Golden Circle" and that they were empowered to receive any number of persons as members of the Order, on the payment of the small fee of five dollars per capita. They represented that the Northern Society was closely connected with a similar society at the South, and that the persons and property of all members would be respected by the Confederate Army. In this way thousands of people were induced to pay their money for the privilege of being accounted as friends of the South; hence our apparently cordial greeting along our line of march. A shrewd Yankee trick that.

Gen. Early destroyed the [railroad] cars and tore up the railroad at York but could not burn the Depot & Government buildings without indangering the town, so he left them standing.[28] I called to see a sister of my deceased friend & brother-in-law, Gen. J. K. Duncan— met with a *frigid* reception. When I rode up to her house the husband darted out of the back door in a painful state of trepidation, leaving his wife to do the honors. After I had remained there for some time, the old man's curiosity got the better of his fears and he returned, and was hugely relieved and rejoiced at finding that my visit was not for a hostile purpose.

June 30. Gen. Lee's objective point was known to be Harrisburg, the capital of the State, and two Divisions of Ewell's Corps (Rodes & Johnson's) were at Carlyle, while Longstreet's Corps was at Chambersburg. As Gen. Lee, with Hill's Corps, descended the eastern slope of the South Mountain, he was surprised to find the head of the Federal Column in his front. Gen. Stuart, instead of marching with his cavalry on the flank of and *pan passer* [?] with [George] Meade's Army,[29] had gone out of his way to capture a large train of

28. In addition to the limited destruction of railroad property in York, Early demanded $100,000, two thousand pairs of shoes, one thousand pairs of socks, one thousand hats, and three days' rations. Although not all his demands were met, Early believed the townspeople tried to comply and so left them unmolested. *OR,* Vol. XXVII, Pt. II, 464–68.

29. Major General George Gordon Meade, Spanish-born and a West Point graduate, first led a division and then the V Corps in the Army of the Potomac. After Hooker's failure at

the enemy's waggons and had failed to keep Gen. Lee advised of the movements of Meade. Hence the surprise of our General.[30] The position of the Federal Army menaced our communications with the Potomac and Gen. Lee resolved to concentrate his army and give battle where he was. Accordingly, Longstreet came down in all haste from Chambersburg & Ewell from Carlisle. We left York at daylight, passing through the town of Berlin, & camped at dark. Distance, *22 miles*.

From this retrograde movement it was evident to the dullest comprehension that a battle was imminent and it was inspiring to see the spirits of our men rise at the prospect of a fight. We all knew that were Meade's Army to be defeated, the roads to Washington, Baltimore & Philadelphia would be open to us.

July 1st. At early dawn we resumed [the] march to Gettysburg. When within a few miles of that place, the heavy booming of cannon told us that the conflict had begun and we pushed on with great rapidity. A. P. Hill had struck the enemy at 10 a.m. and drove him to the range of hills west of the town.[31] Shortly after, Gen. Ewell came up and placed Rodes' Division on the left of Hill's line. The Federals withdrew most of their troops from Hill's front and massed them opposite to Rodes and the fight began in good earnest. While Rodes was contending against these fearful odds—the enemy's cannon enfilading his line & the danger great that he would be obliged

---

Chancellorsville, Meade was given command of the army on June 28, 1863. He remained its commanding general until the end of the war. Warner, *Generals in Blue,* 315–17.

30. Lee did not have any specific plan to attack Harrisburg as Seymour claimed. His general objective was to penetrate Pennsylvania so as to threaten Washington, Philadelphia, and Baltimore. After entering Northern territory, he simply planned to act as events developed. But Seymour was correct in criticizing Stuart's role in the invasion. Lee had ordered his aggressive cavalry commander to stay east of the army to screen it from Meade's force and to provide intelligence on the Yankee movements. But, as usual, Lee left Stuart wide discretion. As a result, Stuart undertook one of his spectacular rides around the Yankee army. But the raid was a disaster for Lee because Stuart became trapped behind Union lines when he encumbered himself with captured booty. Thus Lee entered enemy territory blindly, unable to obtain desperately needed information on Meade's whereabouts. Edwin B. Coddington, *The Gettysburg Campaign: A Study in Command* (New York, 1968), 8–10; Thomas, *Bold Dragoon,* 232–56.

31. On June 30, James J. Pettigrew's brigade, of Hill's Corps, was dispatched to Gettysburg in search of supplies. Noticing federals of undetermined strength in town, Pettigrew withdrew to inform his superiors. On July 1, Henry Heth's division returned at 10:00 A.M. and collided with Union cavalry west of town. Within hours more units were drawn into the fight and a major battle raged west and northwest of town. Coddington, *Gettysburg Campaign,* 263–66, 286.

to fall back—our Division came up and gave him much needed relief. Gen. Early immediately opened with the artillery upon the batteries that were playing upon Rodes' line and soon silenced them. When within two miles of Gettysburg we formed line of battle across the Berlin Road, with Gordon on our right & Hoke on the left, Smith being left in reserve with the artillery. Gordon was the first to advance. Crossing a small stream under a heavy fire, he encountered a large force that was moving to turn Gen. Rodes' flank. The musketry was very severe and we feared that Gordon would be borne back; but in a few minutes the firing ceased, & the smoke lifting from the field, revealed to our sight the defeated Federals in disorderly flight, hotly pursued by the gallant Georgians. Though this little engagement did not last fifteen minutes, our Pioneers buried *two hundred and twenty-nine of the enemy's dead;* Gordon's loss was *seventy-six in killed and wounded.*[32]

At 4 o'clock P.M., Hays' & Hoke's Brigades were ordered forward against a large force posted nearer the town. On we pushed, driving the enemy in great confusion upon the town, taking whole regiments belonging to the 11th Corps.[33] One Dutch Colonel at the head of about 250 men came up to me and cried out that he surrendered, evidently wishing to get from under fire as soon as possible. I made him throw his sword on the ground and sent the whole party back to our rear guard under the escort of only one Confederate soldier. I knew well enough that they could not escape on the way.

The Federals made a stand at the edge of the town, where they posted two guns to sweep the road up which a portion of our Brigade was advancing. Though the fire of artillery and infantry was very severe at times, it did not cause our gallant fellows to pause for a moment; but on they swept, capturing the two pieces of cannon and driving the enemy pell mell through and beyond the town. Our loss was very small and our captures amounted to 3,000 prisoners— more men than we had in the charging column.[34] In this charge I

32. Seymour greatly understates Gordon's casualties. The Georgia brigade suffered Lee's highest losses for the day—378, or approximately 30 percent of its force. *Ibid.,* 305, 704.

33. Meade's XI Corps, commanded by Oliver O. Howard, had a large number of men of German origin or descent. It was the same unit routed by Jackson at Chancellorsville and was not highly respected by either army. Faust, *Encyclopedia of the Civil War,* 177–78.

34. Hays's brigade numbered approximately fifteen hundred men at the opening of the battle and on this first day lost seven dead, forty-one wounded, and fifteen missing. General

had a very narrow escape from a shell which burst near my head and almost stunning me; two fragments struck my horse on the head and neck, but only wounded him slightly. At night we remained in line of battle in one of the principal streets in the upper part of the town.

The Yankees fled to a high range of hills [Cemetery and Culp's hills] about one thousand yards beyond Gettysburg, upon which they had one battery of artillery. It was Gen. Ewell's intention (so I heard) to charge and take possession of these Hills before night should close in, and had ordered Johnson's Division to come up and join in the attack—not deeming Early's three Brigades strong enough for the purpose. But Gen. ("Extra Billy") Smith,[35] who had been left two miles out on the Berlin road, mistook some parties of our Cavalry for Yankees and sent word that the enemy were placing artillery in position on the hills to his left which threatened our trains with capture. This report caused Johnson to be ordered to make a detour for the purpose of driving the enemy away from that position. He soon found that Smith's alarm was groundless and resumed his march towards the town, but arrived too late to make the attack before dark. Had it not been for the delay caused by this little circumstance "Cemetery Hill" would undoubtedly have been assaulted and taken, and the great battle of Gettysburg never been fought. Here we all felt the loss of Gen. Jackson most sensibly; had he been alive and in command when we charged through the town, I am sure that he would have given his usual orders under like circumstances, "push on the infantry," and time would not have been afforded the enemy to make their position impregnable. On this occasion I heard many officers and men exclaim, "would that Jackson were here."[36]

Hays supported Seymour's claim concerning the number of prisoners taken. He wrote in his report, "I am satisfied that the prisoners taken . . . by my brigade exceeded in numbers the force under my command." *OR*, Vol. XXVII, Pt. II, 479–80; Inspector General's report, June 19, 1863, in Jubal A. Early Papers, 1861–65, War Record Group 109, Entry 118, National Archives.

35. Brigadier General William Smith earned his nickname while serving as a mail coach operator before the war and receiving extra pay for mileage. Faust, *Encyclopedia of the Civil War*, 698.

36. Ewell's failure to attack Cemetery Hill on the afternoon of July 1 was one of several Confederate mistakes at Gettysburg. Lee simply instructed Ewell to advance against Cemetery Hill if he could do so at an advantage. Although a competent commander, Ewell certainly was not as aggressive as Jackson and decided to wait for Johnson's division before at-

Distance marched this day, *12 miles.*

July 2d. Before daylight our Brigade was moved out of the town of Gettysburg to a position in a field in front & a little to the left of the town—some five hundred yards from "Cemetery Hill." All night long the Federals were heard chopping away and working like beavers, and when day dawned the ridge was found to be crowned with strongly built fortifications and bristling with a most formidable array of cannon. Gen. Ewell, in sending us out to this advanced position, intended forming his general line of battle upon us, nearer to the enemy; but when daylight came, he discovered that it was impracticable to do so. He expressed great anxiety to withdraw our Brigade, but this could not be done without an immense loss in face of the powerful batteries on the hill which could sweep, at short range, the field over which we would have to pass in retiring. So we had to remain there—more than five hundred yards in advance of Ewell's line of battle—hugging the ground behind a very low ridge which only partially covered us from the enemy's fire. It was almost certain death for a man to stand upright and we lost during the day forty-five men in killed and wounded from the fire of the enemy's sharpshooters, who were armed with long ranged Whitworth rifles[37] that would kill at a distance of twelve hundred yards.

The Federal line of battle now extended along the crest of a range of high hills in the form of a crescent; in front of this, and on an inferior range, the Confederate line was formed; Ewell's Corps on the left, Hill's in the centre and Longstreet's on the right. Our Division (Early's) occupied the centre of our corps; Johnson's was on our left and consequently on the extreme left of Gen. Lee's line. Preparations were made for an attack upon both wings of the enemy simultaneously, while A. P. Hill was to engage his attention in the centre to prevent them from sending off reinforcements to the threatened points.[38]

---

tacking. As it turned out, Johnson arrived too late and the Confederates lost their best opportunity to dislodge Meade from the strategic hill. *OR,* Vol. XXVII, Pt. II, 444–46.

37. In the mid-1850s, Englishman Sir Joseph Whitworth produced a .45 caliber percussion cap rifle that, when fitted with a long telescopic sight, was capable of killing a man at fifteen hundred to eighteen hundred yards. Faust, *Encyclopedia of the Civil War,* 823.

38. Dismayed at Ewell's failure to complete the Confederate victory on July 1, Lee planned for Longstreet to open the second day's fighting by attacking the area around Little

At four o'clock in the afternoon one of our battalions of artillery appeared on a high hill in rear of the left wing of our Division and boldly opened upon the powerful Yankee batteries in our front. The contest was a very unequal one, the Federals bringing at least fifty pieces to bear upon our eighteen guns; their guns were protected by earth works while ours were placed on the bald top of the hill with no covering of any kind to guns or men. But the gallant young commander of the Confederate batteries, Major [Joseph W.] Latimer, maintained the fight for fully one hour, though suffering terribly in men and horses, and being very severely wounded himself. We could very distinctly see the opposing parties to this terrible "artillery duel" and a most exciting and thrilling spectacle it was. The roar of the guns was continuous and deafening; the shot and shell could be seen tearing through the hostile batteries, dismounting guns, killing and wounding men and horses, while ever and anon an ammunition chest would explode, sending a bright column of smoke far up towards the heavens. I saw the brave little Latimer (he was only 21 years old) sitting quietly on his horse amid this tempest of shot and shell, calmly directing the fire of his guns; but, alas! a shell presently explodes over him and down go horse and rider, the first dead and the other wounded. The Major's leg being caught under the prostrate horse and pinned to the earth, he would not permit the cannoneers to leave their pieces to extricate him; but cooly lay there giving his orders until seeing the futility of prolonging the fight, he commanded his batteries to retire. He was then taken off the field and a few days after yielded up his noble spirit to the God that gave it. A more modest, unassuming Christian gentleman never lived; a more gallant, fearless soldier never died on the battle field than young Latimer.[39]

Round Top, a crucial hill anchoring Meade's left. When Ewell heard Longstreet's attack commence he was to send Johnson's division against Culp's Hill and Early against Cemetery Hill on Meade's right. Rodes's division, on Early's right, was to join in as a supporting force. But Longstreet did not begin his attack until late afternoon, thus throwing Lee's plans awry. Foote, *Civil War,* II, 488–89.

39. When Latimer heard Longstreet's attack begin, he opened fire with his battery to apply pressure on Meade's right. The young officer, whom one Louisiana officer called "our little Napoleon," was mortally wounded when his arm was torn off by a shell. His bloodied battery was then forced to retire. *Ibid.,* 515; Jackson to Jackson, July 20, 1863, in Boyd Civil War Papers.

Soon after the subsidence of this artillery storm, the sharp rattle of musketry on our extreme left showed that Johnson had commenced work and we knew that the time would soon come for us to storm the steep hill and frowning batteries in our front. The quiet, solemn mien of our men showed plainly that they fully appreciated the desperate character of the undertaking, but [on] every face was most legibly written the firm determination to do or die. Just before dark the solitary figure of old Gen. Early is seen emerging from one of the streets of the town and, riding slowly across the field in the direction of our position, the little puffs of dust that arise from around his horse's feet show that the Federal sharpshooters are paying him the compliment of their special attention. Presently the old General reaches us and after inquiring whether we are ready, gives the order to charge.

At the word, up spring our men and away they rush over the little ridge behind which they had so long laid and down into the valley which separated it from the dreaded "Cemetery Hill."[40] The Yankees have anticipated this movement and now thirty pieces of cannon vomit forth a perfect storm of grape, cannister, shrapnel, etc., while their infantry pour into us a close fire from their rifles. But we are too quick for them and are down in the valley in a trice, while the Yankee missiles are hissing, screaming & hurtling over our heads, doing but little damage. Skirting the base of the Hill is a stone-wall, from behind which a heavy line of Yankee infantry greet us with a destructive volley, and many of our noble fellows go down before it killed or wounded. But our little command is not delayed by this impediment more than a minute; the Yankees are easily driven away and up the Hill we go, and, after a short struggle, the much coveted crest and to now silent batteries are ours. We captured here several artillery flags and guidons.

Gen. Hays immediately reformed his line and anxiously waited to hear Rodes' guns co-operating with us on the right; but, unfortu-

40. In the attack on Cemetery Hill, Hays was given command of Robert Hoke's North Carolina brigade. These two brigades knew how dangerous their task was, and Lieutenant Joseph Jackson of Hays's brigade wrote, "I felt as if my doom was sealed and it was with great reluctance that I started my skirmishers forward." Jackson to Jackson, July 20, 1863, in Boyd Civil War Papers.

nately, no such assistance came to us. A few minutes after we had effected a lodgement on the Hill, a column of the enemy came up— it being very dark—to within twenty feet of our line; our men delivered their fire full in the faces of the enemy and the Yankee line melted away in the darkness. Soon after, another and heavier line was discovered in our front, while two columns were heard advancing upon our flanks, threatening to surround and capture our little Brigade and the few men of Hoke's Brigade who charged with us. Gen. Hays, perceiving the imminent danger he was in and having given up all hope of a supporting force coming to his rescue, was obliged to give up his hard earned captures and marching by the right flank he led his Brigade back towards the town, where we remained all night. Had it not been for the darkness, which concealed our movement, the enemy would have, no doubt, cut us up terribly with his re-captured artillery as we fell back from the Hill.

By this evening's fighting we lost three hundred and thirty-two (332) men in killed and wounded;[41] among the former were: Lt. Col. Lewis and Capt. [Victor] St. Martin, of the 8th Regt.; Major Williams and Adjutant [Richard T.] Crawford, of the 9th; Lieut. [Wallace P.] Talbot, of the 7th; Capt. [Louis A.] Cormier,[42] of the 6th; and Capt. [Frederick] Richardson, of the 5th. This charge was a daring and desperate one and, although unsuccessful on account of the failure of our supports to come up, we gained great credit for it. It was afterwards reported that Gen. Rodes had advanced only half way to the Hill, when discovering that the Division on his right (one of A. P. Hill's) was not supporting him, he halted and left us to go on alone.[43]

41. Seymour must be referring to the total casualties in both brigades. Hays officially listed his casualties at 21 dead, 119 wounded, and 41 missing. Hoke lost 13 dead, 93 wounded, and 94 missing. *OR*, Vol. XXVII, Pt. II, 480–82, 484.

42. In a postwar newspaper article, Seymour wrote that Cormier was shot in the stomach while leading his company against Cemetery Hill. The next day several Gettysburg women came to the barn used as Hays's field hospital to help with the Confederate wounded. They were touched by Cormier, and he asked them to come by later to see him die. They did, and he thanked them before passing away. Undated newspaper clipping in Seymour Papers.

43. Hays had attacked and briefly captured the Union batteries of Captains Bruce Ricketts and Michael Wiedrich, supported by the XI Corps' 1st Division. Seymour's description of Rodes's action is somewhat in error. Ewell had expected Rodes to support Hays on the right, but Rodes had not completed deploying his troops when it came time for the assault—thus Rodes failed to support it. But Seymour is correct in mentioning that Hays's brigade received accolades for its daring attempt. Some soldiers even believed the Louisiana general might be promoted to major general for the way he handled his men at Gettysburg. And several

On the extreme right two of Longstreet's Brigades charged the enemy's works, capturing a portion of them, but were forced to retire on account of the failure of their supports. This want of concert of action on the part of our Generals was the chief cause of the loss of the great battle of Gettysburg and made Gen. Lee remark, reproachfully, that his Generals could not expect him to be at all points on the battle field at the same time. The Army was fought by Divisions instead of by Corps, which was a great and most unfortunate mistake.[44]

July 3d. In line of battle in one of the streets of Gettysburg, where we remained all day. Heavy skirmishing going on in front of the town, but no general attack made along our portion of the line. Precisely at noon commenced the greatest "artillery duel" of the war. In front of Longstreet's left and Hill's right, Gen. Lee had massed one hundred and thirty-five pieces of artillery, which at a given signal opened upon the enemy's centre. The Federals responded with over two hundred guns and for four hours the earth shook with the thunder of these terrible engines of war.[45] Naught could be heard but the hoarse roar of the cannon, the screaming and bursting of shell, the dull *thud* of the solid shot as it buried itself in the ground, the crash of falling timber, the loud explosion of amunition chests, the uneart[h]ly cries of wounded horses, and the loud shouts of defiance of the combatants. It was a most terrible scene and made one believe that truly "Hell was empty, and all the devils were there."

---

writers claimed that the attack came close to altering history. Union general Carl Schurz wrote, "The fate of the battle might hang on the repulse of this attack," and historian Douglas Southall Freeman claimed, "The whole of the three days' battle produced no more tragic might-have-been than the twilight engagement on the Confederate left." Freeman, *R. E. Lee,* III, 102; Carl Schurz, *The Reminiscences of Carl Schurz* (3 vols.; New York, 1907–1908), III, 24; *OR,* Vol. XXVII, Pt. II, 319–20, 556, 715, 722.

44. Seymour rightly criticizes the Confederates for fighting piecemeal at Gettysburg, but ultimate responsibility for the defeat rests with Lee. As usual, he decided on the general battle plan and then left it up to his subordinates to work out the details of timing, positioning of troops, and so on. This strategy usually worked well with Jackson at the helm of the II Corps, but at Gettysburg Ewell and Hill were leading their corps in battle for the first time. Thus Lee should have been more careful to see that his plans were effectively carried out. Incidents like Rodes's failure to join in the attack on July 2 were representative of the entire Confederate effort at Gettysburg. Freeman, *R. E. Lee,* III, 82–85, 92.

45. After both attacks on Meade's flanks failed on July 2, Lee decided to assault the Union center on July 3 with George Pickett's and Henry Heth's divisions. To soften up the Union line for his 13,500 men, Lee opened an artillery barrage at 1:00 P.M. (not noon) with approximately 175 guns. The federals replied with about 120 pieces. *OR,* Vol. XXVII, Pt. II, 320–21; Coddington, *Gettysburg Campaign,* 458–64, 486, 493–534.

A few minutes after 4 o'clock P.M. another and final attempt was made to take the Heights occupied by the Yankees. [George] Pickett's splendid Division, of Longstreet's corps, marched forward to the attack; [Henry] Heth's Division [Hill's Corps], commanded by [James] Pettigrew,[46] being ordered to support it. Just as Pickett got within easy range of the enemy's batteries, our artillery, unfortunately, ceased firing from exhaustion of their amunition and the Yankee artillerists were enabled to bestow their whole attention upon Pickett's line of attack.[47] In spite of the great rents made in their ranks by the enemy's shot and shell, Pickett's gallant Virginians steadily advanced, and charging up the Hill planted their banners on the Yankee works. Had Pettigrew come up at this time the day would have been won. That General's Division as it came across the plateau under the withering fire of the enemy's guns, quailed and fell back in confusion; it was composed, for the most part, of raw troops and no orders, threats or entreaties could induce them to again face the iron storm. This failure of his supporting column forced Pickett to abandon the captured works and fall back to his original line; executing this movement, his losses were terribly severe, everyone of his Brigadiers being wounded and only two out of twenty-four field officers escaping unhurt. This charge was considered one of the most brilliant of the war.[48]

This was the grand closing scene of the bloody drama of Gettysburg. Gen. Lee was forced to the conclusion that the enemy's

46. Henry Heth had been badly wounded during the first day's fighting so Brigadier General James J. Pettigrew of North Carolina took temporary command of the division and advanced on Pickett's left. Warner, *Generals in Gray*, 133, 237–38.

47. Lee had ordered his chief of artillery to try to knock out the federal guns during the bombardment and to inform Longstreet to begin the assault when he believed he had succeeded. The federals realized an infantry attack was coming, however, and slackened their fire to save ammunition. When the enemy counterfire ceased, the Confederate artillerymen believed they had succeeded in their task and the attack began. Although low ammunition supplies influenced the Confederate decision, the main reason for the order to cease fire was this mistaken belief that the Confederate bombardment had silenced the enemy batteries. Coddington, *Gettysburg Campaign*, 496–501.

48. It was true that part of Pettigrew's force failed to keep up with Pickett's division, but the main reason was the organization of the attack. The Confederates placed their brigades along a broad front rather than forming a compact force with depth for support. When Pettigrew's left flank was hit hard by artillery and musketry, there were no reserves for it to fall back on, so it fled the field. Still, it is doubtful whether the attack would have succeeded. Pickett's Charge was not, as Seymour claimed, a brilliant attack, although the rebels' courage was awe-inspiring. Lee vastly overestimated what his men could accomplish and suffered a stunning defeat. For once, the Army of Northern Virginia was simply outfought. *Ibid.*, 460–61, 489–90, 506–508, 514.

position was impregnable and resolved to withdraw his troops. At the battle of Gettysburg our loss was ten thousand men. The enemy's was, according to their own accounts, about fifteen thousand[49]—their crowded ranks on the Hill having suffered greatly from the fire of our artillery.

During the day Gen. Ewell, accompanied by Major [Captain H. B.] Richardson, his Chief of Engineers, rode past our Brigade and started on a little reconnoitring tour on a road that entered the town where our left rested. We told him that it was dangerous to go out that road—that the enemy's sharpshooters commanded it with their long-ranged, telescopic sighted Whitworth rifles. The old General declared that they were fully fifteen hundred yards distant—that they could not possibly shoot with accuracy at that distance & that he would run the risk of being hit. He had not proceeded twenty paces when a ball perforated his wooden leg and Major Richardson was shot through the body.[50]

July 4th. Moved before dawn with the whole army and formed line of battle on a ridge one mile to the right of the town, where we remained all day. When day broke our pickets reported Meade's Army retreating—in fact both armies were withdrawing at the same time. But when Meade discovered that Gen. Lee had merely fallen back to another position, he marched his men back to the works on the heights.[51] This being the "glorious Fourth," we thought the Yankees would burn great quantities of harmless gunpowder in honor of the day; but they had suffered too much to indulge in any such jubilation, so they spent the day in burying their dead. Gen. Lee at this time gave the Federal General a fine opportunity of attacking him, but it was declined. Gen. Lee had only amunition enough for only two days' hard fighting—was far distant from his depots of supply—and, consequently, was obliged to put himself on the defensive.[52]

July 5th. Left position at 2 a.m. and marched in the direction of

49. Actual Confederate casualties were 20,451 and for the federals, 23,049. *Ibid.*, 536, 541.
50. One of Ewell's aides placed this incident on July 2. Campbell Brown, "Reminiscences of the Civil War," in Campbell Brown Collection, Southern Historical Collection, University of North Carolina, Chapel Hill.
51. Actually, Meade never retreated on July 4. He remained in position ready to receive another attack from Lee. Coddington, *Gettysburg Campaign*, 535–47.
52. Seymour puts the best light on Lee's decision to retreat after the battle. After the slaughter of Pickett's Charge, Lee knew his only chance to salvage a victory was if Meade

South Mountain, halting now and then to see if the Yankee Army would come out and give us battle. At one time during the day, when the enemy showed some signs of pursuing, Gen. Lee halted our Corps—which was bringing up the rear—and told Gen. Ewell to try to induce the enemy to fight. The old General remarked that "if 'those people' will only come out of their entrenchments and give us an open field fight, we will *smash* them." I never saw Gen. Lee so anxious for a fight. Our Division was the rear guard of the army and had lively skirmishing during the afternoon with the enemy's cavalry and flying artillery. Bivouacked at night near Fairfield, at the entrance to the gap in the South Mountains. Distance marched, *6 miles*.

July 6th. Resumed the march at daylight & crossed the Mountains, bivouacking at night at our old camping ground near Waynesboro. On the Mountain road we passed the wrecks of several wagons and ambulances, which the Yankee Cavalry had destroyed a few days before in an attack upon our train. During the battle of Gettysburg, a report was generally current that our whole train had been captured, but it proved to be greatly exaggerated, as only thirty or forty wagons were destroyed, when the enemy were driven off and severly punished. Distance *15 miles*.

July 7th. Left Waynesboro at daybreak and marched to within two miles of Hagerstown, Md., where we remained in camp for the two following days. *Distance, 11 miles.*

July 11th. Army formed line of battle—men busy all day in fortifying. Here we remained until the night of the 13th in momentary expectation of the enemy's advance. There was considerable skirmishing by our Cavalry in our front. Gen. Lee's position covered the Potomac from Williamsport to Falling Waters. Early on the morning of the 12th the enemy appeared in heavy force in our front and proceeded to fortify. We were all very anxious to have the Yankees attack us, for our position was a very strong one and we felt perfectly confident that we could defend it successfully. But Gen. Meade showed no inclination to hazard another general engagement—keeping quiet in his entrenchments, evidently awaiting

---

attacked his reinforced position. When Meade refused, Lee had no choice but to retreat to Virginia. *Ibid.,* 535.

the opportunity of striking our column when it should attempt to cross the Potomac. After remaining here for three days, and his whole train having safely passed to the other side of the river, Gen. Lee made preparations to cross over with the Army.

July 13. At dark marched to Williamsport. At 4 o'clock next morning the Brigade crossed the River on a pontoon Bridge—the General (Hays) and I crossed on a scow. *Distance, 10 miles.*

The passage of the Potomac was a very hazardous undertaking; the waters were very high, and the crossing was effected in the face of a watchful and powerful enemy. But it was accomplished with no loss of material except a few disabled wagons & two pieces of cannon which the horses were unable to drag through the deep mud. The Yankee Cavalry made a dash at our rear guard, killing Gen. Pettigrew & capturing some twenty or thirty men—a most insignificant loss when we consider the magnitude and hazardous nature of the movement. The rain descended in torrents during the whole night and we all were soaked through to the skin.

July 15th & 16th. On the march. Arrived at Darksville on the evening of the 16th—went into camp and remained there until the 20th. *Distance, 17 miles.*

July 20th. Left camp at 7 P.M. and marched to the foot of North Mountain. Distance, *5 miles.*

July 21st. At daylight resumed the march and proceeded to the village of Hedgesville to fight a heavy force of Yankees, under Genl. Mulligan, reported near that place. Before we reached them, our advance guard of cavalry reported that the birds had taken wings and fled towards Romney. Though our march was rapidly executed, Gen. Mulligan had received information concerning it from a "loyal" Union man who had observed the movement of troops and hastened to impart the information to his Yankee friends.[53] Our men were halted in an immense field of black berries, in which the whole Division regaled themselves. The troops declared that it was

53. It is unclear to whom Seymour is referring. There was no General Mulligan in the Union army. He is probably referring to Brigadier General Benjamin Franklin Kelley, the Union general in charge of protecting the Baltimore and Ohio Railroad. Ewell's Corps was ordered on July 20 to capture Kelley's force near Hedgesville, but the federals escaped. *OR,* Vol. XXVII, Pt. II, 449–50, 472; Faust, *Encyclopedia of the Civil War,* 410; Jackson to Jackson, July 20, 1863, in Boyd Civil War Papers.

merely a foraging expedition and that Gen. Early had marched them there to draw rations of blackberries—rations of bread and meat being quite scanty in camp. Distance marched, *23 miles.*

July 22d. Marched to Bunker Hill. *16 miles.*

July 23d. Passed through Winchester. *16 miles.*

July 24th.   ''   ''   Strasburg—*25 miles.*

   '' *25th.* Marched to within four miles of Mt. Jackson. *19 miles.*

   '' *26th.*   ''   ''   New Market. *11 miles.*

   '' *27th.* Crossed the Massanutten Mountain and camped at [the] foot of [the] Blue Ridge near Hawksville. Distance marched, *16 miles.* Though the mountain is only about one mile and a half high, the winding, zigging road to the top over which we passed is nearly eight miles long. From the summit a very extendid and magnificent view of the Shenandoah and Luray Valleys can be obtained.

July 28th. Crossed the Blue Ridge at Fisher's Gap and marched *20 miles.*

July 29th. Marched to Madison Court House, where we camped, remaining there during the following day. *Distance, 7 miles.*

July 31st. Proceeded to vicinity of Locust Dale, on Robertson River, *11 miles.*

August 1st. Crossed Robertson and Rapidan Rivers, camping three miles from the last named, half a mile from Clark's Mountain and seven miles from Orange Court House. Remained here until September 14th.

RAPPAHANNOCK STATION AND
MINE RUN

THE Gettysburg Campaign had shattered both armies. As a result, active campaigning was suspended during the latter part of the summer as each side took time to rest and refit. While Lee pondered his next move, Seymour and the 1st Louisiana Brigade spent several weeks at Raccoon Ford on the Rapidan River, picketing and skirmishing with the Yankees. During this lull, Lee was finally persuaded to send Longstreet's corps to Georgia in an attempt to bolster faltering Confederate efforts in the West. But the inactivity was brief, and cooler weather brought renewed efforts by the antagonists. When Lee discovered that Meade had also weakened his army by sending a force westward, he decided it was time to strike. There followed a flurry of activity in October and November, 1863, as Lee and Meade maneuvered for position. For Seymour it proved to be an autumn full of hardships as he watched his men march barefoot over the rough Virginia roads and at times endure bitterly cold weather. Even worse, the suffering led not to victory but to disaster along the banks of the Rappahannock.

September 14th, 1863. Broke camp at 7 o'clock in the morning and proceeded to Somersville Ford on the Rapidan. Upon our arrival there we discovered the enemy's Cavalry having a spirited fight with our Cavalry pickets on the other side of the River; the enemy far outnumbering them, our Cavalry retired to this side of the River and took post at Raccoon Ford, three miles below Somersville. At 11 A.M., we marched to Raccoon Ford and relieved the Cavalry Brigade of Gen. [James Byron] Gordon, of North Carolina. In doing this the 5th, 7th & 8th Regts. had to cross a ravine and ascend a precipitous hill near the River, were greatly exposed to the enemy's fire of artillery posted on the opposite bank, and we lost several men in killed and wounded in the execution of the movement. Our Brigade soon got into position and drove the Yankee artillery away. Brisk skirmishing continued all day between our pickets and those of the enemy concealed in and behind houses on the other side of the Rapidan.[1]

Sept. 15th. Skirmishing resumed at daylight and continued all day—the Brigade occupying a position on the high banks about the Ford. The enemy had two large Divisions of Cavalry, commanded by [Judson] Killpatrick and [John] Buford on the opposite side of the River, and by their display of force and maneuvering showed a disposition to attack us and force the passage of the Rapidan. But the day wore away without such an attempt being made. The evolution of the Yankee Cavalry—seven thousand in number—which was made in a broad, open field, was a very imposing spectacle; they seemed strong enough to ride over our little Brigade, only a thousand strong, but we had the superior position and Gen. Killpatrick wisely concluded not to make the effort.

Sept. 16th. Skirmishing continued. At 2 o'clock P.M. two companies of volunteers—one from the 5th and one from the 9th Regt.—under command of Capt. Frank Moore,[2] of the 5th Regt., crossed the River a short distance below Raccoon Ford and made a dash at some houses in which the enemy's reserve pickets were posted. The surprise was complete and Capt. Moore's party killed and wounded twelve Yankees, and captured 42 cavalrymen of the 5th New York (a crack Regiment), including a Captain and three Lieutenants. The Major Commanding the Regt., who happened to be visiting the outpost at the time, was killed. His death was greatly lamented by those of his officers and men whom our party captured, and they accused our men of killing him after he had surrendered; but this accusation was false. Being surprised in one of the houses aforementioned, one of our officers ordered him to surrender, to which

1. This clash with federal cavalry occurred as Meade probed Lee's defenses of the Rapidan fords. *OR,* Vol. XXIX, Pt. I, 111–19.
2. Captain Frank L. Moore, a former steamboatman, had a fascinating military career. He enlisted as a substitute for another man in June, 1861, and was jailed for mutiny in September. Nevertheless, he was promoted from private to first lieutenant in December. Moore was wounded at Second Manassas and gained a promotion to captain in October, 1862. Booth, comp., *Records of Louisiana Confederate Soldiers,* Vol. III, Book II, 1030.

he replied by discharging his pistol, whereupon he was immediately shot down. Killpatrick was so chagrined at this little raid that he had the colors taken away from the Regiment, a detachment of which was thus surprised.[3] Moore did not lose a man. Considering that his force consisted of forty men and that the enemy's line of battle was only about six hundred yards distant from the outpost, this little affair was a brilliant one & Moore was highly complimented by his superiors.

Sept. 17th & 18th. Occasional picket firing during the day. No demonstration in force by the enemy. Commenced raining at 2 o'clock P.M. on the 11th and rained until 1 P.M. next day.

Sept. 19th. No firing today. Commenced making entrenchments. One brass Napolean gun was placed immediately on the River bank and three pieces of cannon were mounted on the hill overlooking the Ford. Raccoon [F]ord being the most important one on the River, everything was done that labor and science could accomplish to make it impassable to the enemy. Nothing of interest occurred along our front during the following four days.

Sept. 24th. All quiet along our front, but heavy columns of enemy are seen from the Signal Station on Clark's Mountain to be moving in the direction of Germania Ford—ten miles below us—which induces the belief that an early attack will be made upon our lines.

Sept. 25th. Enemy reported in line of battle in front of Germania Ford, and the supposition is that he intends crossing the River and to make the attempt to turn our right flank. As yet we have but a few Cavalrymen to oppose him at that point. I think that Gen. Lee has left that Ford thus weakly defended for the purpose of inducing the Yankees to cross and attack him at that point.[4]

Sept. 26th & 27th. Movements of the enemy noticed on the other side of the River and we are on the *qui vive* for an attack. But everything remained quiet this & the following day.

Sept. 28th. At 10 o'clock A.M., when the fog had cleared away,

3. Seymour is in error about the Union regiment's identity. Official records show it was the 4th New York Cavalry but do not mention what losses it sustained in the incident. *OR*, Vol. XXIX, Pt. I, 114.

4. Lee apparently did not view these maneuvers as a real threat, calling them a reconnaissance in force, and never mentioned any plans to entice the Yankees to attack him. *Ibid.*, 134–35.

the enemy was seen from Clark's Mountain to be in line of battle; our troops were quickly placed under arms and the works manned. This movement on the part of the Yankees turned out to be a review of the whole army for the benefit of Abe Lincoln. They seemed to be much disturbed by our preparations and display of force, and their immense wagon park at Mitchell's Station broke up in great haste and moved off at a double quick in the direction of Culpepper Court House.

Oct. 5th. Brigade under arms on account of the enemy's being reported as advancing towards the River. A mere feint on the part of Gen. Meade.

Oct. 8th. Gen. Lee by this time has discerned that his Yankee antagonist has abandoned the intention of attacking him in his stronghold on the Rapidan line and, though having but two corps with him (Ewell's & Hill's), has resolved to make a grand & daring flank movement and place his Army between Meade and the Potomac.[5] At 6 P.M. received orders to move; Brigade marched at 7 P.M. two miles and halted for the night. Relieved at Raccoon Ford by two Regiments of Gordon's Brigade.

Oct. 9th. Moved at sunrise and marched to Orange Court House (fourteen miles); thence to four miles beyond the Rapidan (crossing the River one mile above Barnett's Ford) where we bivoucked for the night.

Oct. 10th. Marched (at sunrise) to Robinson's River—11 miles—crossed it and camped seven miles from the Ford.

Oct. 11th. Started one hour by sun and marched fifteen miles to within six miles of Culpepper & to the west of the town. Camped at 7 P.M.

Oct. 12th. Marched to the Rappahannock (15 miles), crossed the River and camped three miles beyond. Brisk firing was heard on our right during the day, where Stuart is driving before him Killpatrick's troopers.[6]

5. Following Gettysburg, Lee acquiesced to temporarily transferring Longstreet's corps to assist Braxton Bragg's army in Georgia. He was too weak for offensive action until he learned that Meade had also dispatched two corps to Georgia. Lee then took the offensive. By marching north and west, Lee hoped to outflank Meade's position, force him to withdraw, and then strike the Yankee army while it was off balance. Freeman, *R. E. Lee,* III, 169–70; Foote, *Civil War,* II, 786.

6. As planned, Meade began retreating when Lee advanced. Stuart's cavalry preceded

Oct. 13th. Moved at daybreak and reached Warrenton Springs at sun rise, where we rested for one hour. On either side of the roads leading to and from this place were a number of dead Yankees and dead horses, the results of a fight the night before between some of A. P. Hill's infantry and a Division of Federal Cavalry. Resuming the march, we reached Warrenton at 10 o'clock A.M. Camped two miles from town and went to work cooking rations.

Gen. Stuart, intent upon driving before him Killpatrick's troopers to prevent them from discovering the movement of our Army, had unfortunately gotten his Cavalry Corps at night between two heavy columns of the enemy's infantry moving on parallel roads. Meade, at first, thought that Gen. Lee intended fighting him on the Rappahannock and massed his army in that vicinity; but finding that Lee was marching still farther North, he put his army in motion and was now moving rapidly, by night and day, to outstrip the Confederates in the race for Centreville. One of the roads along which the Yankee army was moving ran within only seven miles of Warrenton and had it not been for Stuart's mishap Gen. Lee would have obtained from him exact information of its whereabouts, which would have enabled him to place himself in front of Meade & between him and Bull Run. Not hearing from Stuart, Gen. Lee remained at Warrenton until the following morning.

Oct. 14th. Information of Stuart's critical situation having been received by means of two of his men penetrating the enemy's lines and reaching Gen. Lee's Head Quarters before daylight, our Corps was ordered forward to extricate him. Broke camp at 5 o'clock A.M. and had not marched three miles before our forces were engaged. Our Brigade was carried to the extreme left of the Corps and formed in line of battle in support of Gordon's Brigade. We advanced some distance with Gordon, when the enemy fell back under cover of his artillery, of which he had a powerful force. Gen. Stuart was thus enabled to get out of his unpleasant and dangerous predicament.[7]

---

the army to screen it from the federals and was often engaged with Kilpatrick's division. Thomas, *Bold Dragoon,* 264–67.

7. After becoming trapped between the two federal columns, Stuart hid his men in a secluded valley and sent word of his predicament to Lee. Lee had Ewell make a demonstration with his corps at dawn, at which time Stuart was able to cut his way out to safety. *Ibid.;* Freeman, *R. E. Lee,* II, 169–87.

By this time most of Meade's army had passed and we were engaged with the 5th Corps, which brought up the rear. The Yankee General showed no disposition to halt his army and give us battle, but continued his march with great celerity towards Bull Run, behind which stream he seemed very anxious to get posted. Gen. Lee was, no doubt, greatly disappointed at this non-combative disposition manifested by his antagonist, for "Marse Robert" had evidently started out with the determination to draw Meade into a fight on equal ground.

The army was then hastened on towards Bristow Station, where our Division arrived at 5 o'clock in the afternoon. Hill's Corps, moving on the shorter road on our left, was in advance and struck the enemy first at the Station. Hill was in such a hurry to anticipate Ewell and attack first that he sent forward only two Brigades ([Philip] Cook's & [William W.] Kirtland's [Kirkland's]) to attack a whole Corps of the enemy posted in a railroad cut & having a heavy force of artillery on a commanding hill behind it. These small Brigades advanced with great boldness and intrepidity, and charged up to within a few yards of the Yankee line, but were badly cut up and scattered in confusion by the vastly superior numbers opposed to them. The Yankees charged in turn, capturing a battery from Hill which had been left without support. Night coming on, the fighting terminated.[8] We came up shortly after Hill's *fiasco* and, forming on his right, advanced half of a mile, skirmishing a little, but not generally engaged. In line of battle all night. The wounded Confederates and Yankees who remained on the battle field of [the] previous afternoon, screamed and groaned all night, and though we could hear them plainly crying for assistance, we were unable to relieve them owing to the proximity of the enemy's line.

Oct. 15th. The dawn of day revealed to us the unwelcome fact that the enemy had escaped. Our Brigade moved to a position a short distance beyond the station, where we remained for three hours—

---

8. Hill hastily advanced against the Yankees at Bristoe Station because he wanted to hit them while they were in the process of crossing a creek, not, as Seymour claims, to beat Ewell to the attack. But the assault was badly planned. Only the two brigades mentioned were sent in, although others were close at hand. Hill also failed to detect a strong Union force in position behind a nearby railroad embankment. As a result, Hill's men were badly repulsed and humiliated. James I. Robertson, Jr., *General A. P. Hill: The Story of a Confederate Warrior* (New York, 1987), 234–40.

the Yankees having marched all night and esconced themselves behind Bull Run. While we were here, Gen. Lee and Staff came up to a
little knoll a few yards in front of our line. The General seemed to
be in no good humor and casting a glance over the field thickly
strewed with dead Confederates sharply called to Gen. Hill to send
immediately for his pioneer corps to bury his unfortunate dead.
Gen. Hill recognized a rebuke in the tone and manner of his commander and replied, "this is all my fault, General." "Yes," said Lee,
"it is your fault; you committed a great blunder yesterday; your line
of battle was too short, too thin, and your reserves were too far behind." Poor Hill, he appeared deeply humiliated by this speech and
no doubt wished that he could sink out of sight in the lowest depths
of his capacious cavalry boots, and there hide his diminished head.

Our men brought in during the day quite a number of prisoners,
stragglers from the Federal Army, among whom was a deserter
from the Sixth La. Regt. of our Brigade, who was caught in Federal
uniform.

Gen. Lee had failed to interpose his army between that of Meade
and Manassas so he resolved to tear up the [Orange and Alexandria]
railroad, that his expedition should not be entirely barren of result.
To cover this operation he sent forward his Cavalry under Stuart to
Bull Run with orders to skirmish with the enemy and show a bold
front.

Oct. 16th. Camped one mile from the Station—the whole army
engaged in tearing up and bending fourteen miles of rail. Our Brigade destroyed one mile and a quarter of the railroad. Our Corps
had had much experience in this kind of work and the amount of
destruction they affected in a day was remarkable. The process is a
simple one. The rails were first prized up, then the wood work was
taken up; the sleepers and cross-ties were put in piles and the rails
laid across them, the ends projecting over the sides. Fire was then
kindled under each pile; when the wood work would be consumed,
the rails would be burned to a red heat in the middle and the weight
of the projecting ends would cause them to bend, destroying them
for further use. During the last year of the war a machine was invented and used, by which rails bent in this manner could be quickly
straightened and made serviceable.

Oct. 17th. In camp all day and a miserable, damp, dreary day it was. All bare-footed and sick men ordered to proceed to the rear—as far as Catlett's Station—an inevitable prelude to a march; and we are exercising our wits in guessing whether the Army will go in pursuit of Meade or fall back behind the Rappahannock.

Oct. 18th. Broke camp at daylight and marched to within four miles of the Rappahannock. Distance, 16 miles.

Oct. 19th. Resumed march at dawn, our Brigade bringing up the rear of the whole Army. The Yankee Cavalry followed us, but manifested no desire to attack. Crossed the Rappahannock on pontoon bridge and camped one mile from Bridge.

Oct. 20th. Moved camp to within two miles of Brandy Station, where we remained until [the] 23d without anything of interest occuring.

Oct. 23d. The Yankees having appeared on the other side of the River, Gen. Early sent a force over there to drive them away. Left Camp at sun rise with the other Brigades of the Division and crossed the River. Formed line of battle about three miles from the Bridge and advanced against the Yankee force, consisting of two Brigades of Cavalry, supported by one of infantry. We were on the extreme left of the line and went far in advance of the [other] Brigades of the Division. The Yankees, though drawn up in a most imposing line on a commanding ridge of hills, scampered away at our approach. We recrossed the River late in the afternoon and returned to camp.

November 1st. Moved camp to a belt of woods between Brandy [Station] and Culpepper—one mile and a half from the first and four miles from the last named place. Men commenced erecting huts for winter quarters. Here we remained, without anything of interest transpiring, until the 7th inst.[9]

November 6th. At sunrise the Brigade, under command of Col. D[avidson] B. Penn of the 7th Regt.—Gen. Hays being absent on Court of Inquiry—marched to the Bridge, crossed the Rappahannock and relieved the "Stonewall" Brigade (Gen. [James A.] Walker)

9. Upon recrossing the Rappahannock River after the Bristoe Station Campaign, Lee left one pontoon bridge spanning the river where the Orange and Alexandria Railroad crossed at Rappahannock Station. This bridge was left standing so Lee could recross the river for future offensive action. To protect the bridge, Early's and Johnson's divisions took turns picketing the north bank. Jones, *Lee's Tigers,* 181.

of Johnson's Division, which was doing picket duty at that point. Enemy's Cavalry videttes in sight, but no firing between pickets.

Nov. 7th. All quiet until 10½ A.M., when our videttes reported a regiment of the enemy's infantry crossing the railroad, passing down the Warrenton & Fredericksburg Road in the direction of Kelly's Ford; shortly afterwards another force of infantry was discovered marching in the same direction. Col. Penn and I went out to the vidette line to watch the movements of the enemy and we soon discovered that a very heavy force was marching towards our right. As soon as this was found to be the case, the Col. sent a dispatch (which I wrote)—at a quarter to 12 M.—to Gen. Early, informing him that the enemy—both cavalry and infantry—were in our front in very heavy force. The General, with the other Brigades of the Division, was six miles distant. At a quarter past one, I sent another dispatch by order of Col. Penn conveying the information that the Yankees had formed line of battle—that their skirmishers had advanced a short distance and that a large column had moved down the River towards Kelly's Ford, accompanied by wagons and ambulances.[10]

The enemy were formed in a belt of woods one mile & a half from our position. At 2 P.M. the Federals formed another line about two hundred [yards] in advance of the first; half of an hour afterwards they advanced for a quarter of a mile, discovering three lines of battle. This movement revealed to us the overwhelming numbers of the force opposed to us. At 3 ½ P.M., our skirmishers were drawn in and our line formed in the rifle pits immediately about the River & Bridge. The enemy soon got three heavy batteries in position on the high ground in our front and opened upon us a furious fire, most of his shots being aimed at our bridge. At the same time a line of the enemy's skirmishers advanced to within a few yards of the River on our right and poured a heavy fire upon the bridge, for

10. This was the opening phase of Meade's plan to recapture the territory between the Rappahannock and Rapidan rivers. He planned to throw two large columns against Rappahannock Station and Kelly's Ford (five miles downstream) and force Lee to abandon the Rappahannock line. Lee believed the enemy buildup at Rappahannock Station was only a diversion for the main crossing at Kelly's Ford. Therefore, he decided to leave Early's division to hold the bridge and allow the federals to cross below at the ford. Once across the river and away from their supports, Lee would smash the Yankees with Rodes's and Johnson's divisions. Freeman, *R. E. Lee,* III, 189–93; Foote, *Civil War,* II, 799–800.

the double purpose of preventing our retreat and to drive back any re-inforcements that might come to our succor. Under this fire I crossed & recrossed the Bridge four times—8 times in all—bearing orders to the batteries on the other side of the River. Everytime I ascended or descended the hill on the other side, I was greeted by a fusilade from the Yankee skirmishers and the balls whistled around my head in a manner that was not musical in the least. On my last expedition, my noble horse, "Dick Ewell," was wounded in the leg; he lost a large amount of blood, but fortunately had no bones broken. This was his third wound during the war.

At 4½ o'clock, the remainder of the Division came up and Hoke's Brigade, under Col. [Archibald C.] Godwin, immediately crossed the River to our assistance. Unfortunately a sufficient number of troops could not be placed in our entrenchments to successfully resist the powerful force now brought against us—the contracted limits not admitting of more than two small Brigades occupying them; while the ground in front of us was admirably adapted to the concentration of any number of the enemy's troops and to their placing artillery in most favorable and commanding positions.

When our Brigade went on picket and occupied those works, the order transmitted to Col. Penn was to hold the place at all hazards; had it not been for this imperative command, he would, undoubtedly, have withdrawn his troops to the south side of the River and destroyed the Bridge when he found that nearly half of Meade's Army was in his front. The truth is that Genl. Lee's scouts had failed to inform him of Meade's leaving his cantonements around Warrenton and our noble old General was, for once in his life, taken by surprise.[11]

The number of men that Meade brought to the attack was estimated at 20,000 men;[12] we had to oppose them only 1,800 and one battery of artillery, [Capt. Robert] Green's Louisiana Guard Artillery, while two batteries were posted on hills on the South side of the River; these last mentioned batteries gave us very little assistance. The enemy had an unusually heavy skirmish line with three lines of battle, each of which extended far beyond our flanks; on our

11. Lee was not fooled. He knew Meade's army was facing him, but was not expecting a major attack against Rappahannock Station. Freeman, *R. E. Lee*, III, 189–93.

12. Two entire Union corps—the V and VI—faced the fewer than two thousand Confederates on the north bank at Rappahannock Station. *OR*, Vol. XXIX, Pt. I, 557, 587–90.

right a strong force advanced in columns of companies under cover of the railroad bank. The infantry made their principal attack upon our right and centre, and came up without firing a gun; our men fired vigorously, but with coolness and deliberation, and the Yankee skirmishers, as as [sic] they came within easy range of our rifles, melted away before the shower of balls that were poured upon them. Then came the first line of battle and hundreds went down before it had ascended half way up the hill, when, shattered and disorganized, the men laid down and cried out that they surrendered. Closely behind, not twenty paces distant, pressed the second line of Yankees who charged our works with great impetuosity—their daring having been stimulated by a free use of whiskey. Again and again were they hurled back from the trenches, our men fighting most stubbornly with bayonets and clubbed muskets. But the third line coming up, our gallant fellows were overpowered by the sheer weight of numbers and the right and center of our line, upon which the attack was made, was compelled to yield and the enemy poured in yelling like so many demons, many of them being in a state of beastly drunkeness.

As soon as the Yankees got within our works, they formed at right angles with our trenches and marched against our left wing, consisting of the 5th & 7th Regiments and the three regiments of Hoke's Brigade; at the same time heavy masses advanced against the front. Thus hemmed in—it was not quite dark—with a deep, unfordable river in their rear, there was no other alternative left to our Regiments but to surrender. Our loss amounted to six hundred and forty men from Hays' Brigade, about nine hundred from Hoke's Brigade and four pieces of artillery.[13] Among the captured were Col. Penn, of the 7th La.; Capt. [A. L.] Gusman, commanding the 8th Regt.; Capt. [John G.] Angel[l],[14] commanding the 5th Regt. & Col. Godwin comdg. Hoke's Brigade.

Col. [William] Monaghan[15] & Major [William H.] Manning, of the 6th Regt.; Lieut. Col. Terry, of the 7th and Capt. [James] Gar-

13. Hays listed his losses at 2 dead, 16 wounded, and 684 missing; Hoke lost between 900 and 1,000 men. *OR*, Vol. XXIX, Pt. I, 616, 627–29.

14. Penn, Gusman, and Angell remained prisoners until the end of the war. Gusman refused to take the oath of allegiance while in prison and was not released until October, 1865. Booth, comp., *Records of Louisiana Confederate Soldiers*, I, 67, and Vol. III, Book II, 102, 139.

15. Monaghan, a native of Ireland, became commander of the 1st Louisiana Brigade in May, 1864, only to be killed in a skirmish on August 29, 1864. Jones, *Lee's Tigers*, 243.

rity,[16] of the 5th, escaped by swimming the River, as did a number of men. Green's Louisiana Guard battery, commanded by Lieut. [Robert] Moore, fought splendidly, officers & men being captured while serving their guns. Gen. Hays, who came up at 4½ P.M. & assumed command, had a very narrow escape; being at one time surrounded by the enemy, his horse took fright and dashed through the crowd and over the bridge amid a shower of bullets. Col. [William Raine] Peck,[17] of the 9th, and I escaped in the same manner, as did Charley Stuart, one of the couriers, who had his horse struck by by [sic] five balls.[18] I had my horse wounded. This fight was a most unfortunate one for our little Brigade, leaving us with but three hundred and fifty men fit for duty.[19]

At Kelly's Ford, two miles below us, the picket force from Hill's Corps was roughly handled and a number of prisoners taken. Late that night we withdrew to our old camp near Brandy Station.[20]

16. Captain Garrity, who had been wounded at the battles of Malvern Hill and Antietam, was said to have been the only man from the 5th Louisiana to escape death or capture at Rappahannock Station. On company records is written: "He swam the river in which he came very near drowning." He was listed as missing in action in October, 1864, at the Battle of Cedar Creek. Booth, comp., *Records of Louisiana Confederate Soldiers,* II, 979; Compiled Service Records of Confederate Soldiers Who Served in Organizations from the State of Louisiana, War Record Group 109, Microcopy 320, Roll 148, National Archives.

17. Colonel William Raine Peck was a six-feet, six-inch, three-hundred-pound native of Madison Parish, Louisiana. He enlisted as a private but rose through the ranks to become colonel of the 9th Louisiana and was made commander of the brigade in 1864. He was promoted to brigadier general in February, 1865, and was transferred to the western theater. Jones, *Lee's Tigers,* 219, 221.

18. Private Charles Stuart did, indeed, have a narrow escape. A Yankee soldier ordered him off his horse but left him unattended when the federal saw that the horse was wounded and in no shape to ride. But Stuart quickly remounted when the Yankee departed and whipped the bloody horse across the bridge through a hail of gunfire. Peter W. Hairston Diary, Vol. III, November 12, 1863, in Peter W. Hairston Collection, Southern Historical Collection, University of North Carolina, Chapel Hill.

19. The affair at Rappahannock Station was a humiliating defeat for Lee's army. Although the Confederates claimed to have slaughtered the attacking Union forces, the stark truth was that the Yankees had killed or captured over 1,500 rebels at a loss of only 328 men. It was one of the few times Lee was surprised by the Yankees, and his men held him accountable for the disaster, claiming that he either should have sufficiently reinforced Hays or withdrawn him entirely. *Ibid.,* November 10, 12, 1863; Cormier to unknown, November 11, 1863, in Army of Northern Virginia Papers, Part I, Louisiana Historical Association Collection, Tulane University, New Orleans; John McCormick to Marguerite E. Williams, February 2, 1864, in Marguerite E. Williams Collection, Southern Historical Collection, University of North Carolina, Chapel Hill, *OR,* Vol. XXIX, Pt. I, 577, 587–90.

20. Lee's entire plan of action was ruined. Not only had he erred at Rappahannock Station, but the Union column at Kelly's Ford had pounded its way across the river and was closing in on Lee's right rear. His only recourse was to abandon the Rappahannock line and fall back toward the Rapidan. Freeman, *R. E. Lee,* III, 189–93.

Nov. 8th. The enemy commenced crossing the River at daylight and we had to abandon our camp, which we greatly regretted, for it had been admirably selected and laid out, and the huts were more cosy and comfortable than any we had previously built. The Army moved two miles beyond Brandy Station, on the road to Culpepper Court House, [and] formed line of battle. The position was not a good one and Gen. Lee determined to withdraw to his old line behind the Rapidan. At dark we commenced the retrograde movement and proceeded to within three miles of Sommersville Ford, where we bivouacked for the night.

On this day Fitz[hugh] Lee[21] had a smart engagement with the Yankee Cavalry and gained some advantage.

Nov. 9th. Moved at daylight and crossed the Rapidan at Somerville Ford—going into camp one mile from the Ford, where we remained three days.

Nov. 12th. Broke camp and marched to Raccoon Ford, the Brigade picketing at that point—nothing of interest occurring until the 26th inst.

Nov. 26th. Information having been received that Meade had crossed the Rapidan at Germania Ford—twenty miles below us—and was marching in the direction of Locust Grove—with the evident design of getting around Gen. Lee's position and taking possession of the Turnpike and Plank Roads leading from Fredericksburg to Richmond—our army was put in motion to stop "Mr. Meade's" mad carreer.[22]

Left camp at 1 o'clock A.M. and marched a mile beyond Vediersville (8 miles), where we halted for three hours. It was a bitter cold night and we suffered severely during the march. Those of us who were on horseback were so benumbed by the cold that we were compelled to dismount whenever the column halted and dance around on the frozen ground in order to restore circulation. At 8 A.M. [we] proceeded to within one mile of Locust Grove, where

21. Fitzhugh Lee was a nephew of Robert E. Lee and led a division in Stuart's cavalry corps. Warner, *Generals in Gray*, 178–79.

22. In crossing the Rapidan to the east of Lee at Germanna and Ely's fords, Meade planned to hit the roads leading south and west to the Confederates' rear. To counter this movement, Lee took up a new position behind Mine Run, a small stream that formed a natural barrier across Meade's line of advance. Foote, *Civil War*, II, 873–74; *OR*, Vol. XXIX, Pt. I, 825–27.

we met the enemy marching up the Germania road & crossing the one on which we were moving. The enemy had planted a battery in the road on the high hill at the Grove and used it on us quite vigorously, but without doing us any injury. Our Division, which had the advance, withdrew from the road to the woods to prevent the Yankee artillery from raking us as we advanced.

While we were halted for a few minutes, Gen. Lee, mounted on his powerful charger & accompanied by one of his Staff officers, rode up the road, stopping near the head of our Brigade. The old General cooly adjusted his field glasses and sat there, deliberately watching the movement of the enemy's column. The Yankee artillerymen, seeing a mounted officer in the middle of the road only six or seven hundred yards distant, fired shell after shell at him, bursting several of them in dangerous proximity to the General. One shell struck a few yards in front of him and richocheting, passed only some three or four feet over his head; but the noble old hero disregarded it—not even lowering his glasses—and continued his reconnoissance. At last the enemy got the range so perfectly that they exploded a shell right by his side, when yielding to the urgent entreaty of his Staff officer—& having obtained the information he desired—Gen. Lee rode off to another part of the field, much to the relief of those of us who had been watching him with the keenest anxiety. The gallant old General often exposed himself in this manner during a battle, notwithstanding the strong and repeated remonstrances of his subordinate officers. He, like Stonewall Jackson, seemed unwilling in critical emergencies to rely upon the information of others respecting the position & movements of the enemy and would persist in reconnoitring for himself. Jackson lost his life by doing this, but Gen. Lee did not seem to consider his fate as a warning.

By taking advantage of the cover that the woods and the inequality of the ground [provided], our Division moved up some distance and formed line of battle; immediately after[wards] brisk skirmishing commenced, which continued until dark.

Nov. 27. The Yankees having greatly the advantage in position, and we being far in advance of the general line of the Army, at 3 A.M. our Division fell back two miles and commenced fortifying. The enemy advanced by 10 A.M. and opened a heavy fire from his artillery upon our Brigade. This fire showed that our position, which was a salient, could be easily enfiladed; so we fell back at night half a mile, thereby straightening & strengthening the line of battle.

On this day Gen. Edward Johnson's Division, of our Corps, on the extreme left, met and defeated a Federal force under Major Gen. [William] French—consisting of the 3d Corps and one Division of the 5th Corps. The Yankee loss was admitted to be one thousand men—Johnson's was four hundred and fifty. In this fight the enemy attempted to turn our left and capture our wagon train; but they were handsomely foiled by a vastly inferior force. This inauguration of Meade's "on to Richmond" [campaign] was inauspicious and humiliating to the Yankees, and Gen. French was removed from his command for allowing himself to be whipped.[23]

Nov. 28th. About 3 a.m., our Brigade got into its new position and the men set to work with a will to make entrenchments—this making the third line of fortifications they had made within three days. The rapidity with which an army can construct a line of breastworks is truly amazing. When trees are near at hand, they are felled in an inconceivably short space of time, the limbs stripped off, and their trunks are placed lengthwise & on top of each other to the heighth of a man's breast; the interslices are filled with dirt—the whole forming an impenetrable barrier to minie balls and fragments of shell. A top log is often placed on the works, each end resting upon a block, thereby forming a crack of three or four inches through which the men can fire and keep their heads protected by the log. These logs are dangerous when artillery is used against them, for they are liable to be struck by solid shot and rolled over upon the men.

Gen. Lee's position along Mine Run was a very strong one; the ground was high and commanding & the works were more elaborately and substantially made than any our army had previously constructed, while the artillery was massed at prominent points in

23. The Battle of Payne's Farm was not handled well by French. The fight, which largely took place in thick woods, was a surprise to everyone, and French failed to use his superior force effectively. Meade also claimed that French moved his corps too slowly in the Mine Run Campaign and allowed Lee time to prepare a defense. As a result, French lost his corps command when Meade reorganized the army in early 1864. *OR,* Vol. XXIX, Pt. I, 846–49; Faust, *Encyclopedia of the Civil War,* 292, 564.

such a manner as to command all the approaches. This day the Yankees treated us to frequent doses of shot and shell, but made no impression on our works. Our skirmishers kept up a constant and lively fusilade in our front; now and then the Yankees would re-inforce their skirmish line and make an impetuous charge upon ours, but our boys would invariably drive them back with a loud yell. The shouts of the Confederates and of the Yankees are peculiar and distinctive and in a battle it is easy to tell which side is gaining the advantage by noticing the character of the shouts that are given. When elated, the Yankees give regular cheers, like the English, while our fellows, under similar circumstances & also when making a charge, utter the most piercing, irregular, Indian-like yells. These yells, by themselves, have frequently exercised a most *demoralizing* influence upon raw troops in the enemy's line and I have seen, on several occasions, Yankee troops fly the field without firing a shot before the advance of a line of yelling, screaming "Rebs."

We remained in our works until the night of the 1st of December, when Gen. Lee, growing impatient at Meade's hesitation to attack, determined to take the iniative and bring on a general engagement. With this view, he extended the line of Ewell's Corps—now com-manded by Early[24]—so that it occupied the whole line of works—six miles in length—and sent Hill's Corps to make a detour around the left flank of Meade's Army, with instructions to open the fight at daylight. When day dawned on the 2d of December, it was dis-covered that the Federal Army had disappeared from our front & had retreated during the night in the direction of Germania Ford. Our army was quickly put in motion in pursuit after the fugacious Yankees, but they, having had four hours the start of us, were safely across the Rapidan when we arrived at the Ford. We captured four hundred stragglers.

That night we returned to Mine Run and camped for the night. A more ravenously hungry set of mortals never were to be seen than could be found in our Brigade this night. We had been without food for about thirty hours—for twenty of which we had been on the

24. Early temporarily took over the II Corps when Ewell fell ill. This elevated Hays to the command of Early's division during the campaign and Monaghan to the command of the 1st Louisiana Brigade. *OR,* Vol. XXIX, Pt. I, 830–40.

march—and when we reached camp late at night, we found no rations wherewith to appease our appetites. Our commissary wagons had lost their way and we were compelled to go to rest, each vexed and annoyed by that vacuum that Nature so much abhors. On all sides could be heard oft repeated curses, both loud and deep, as our men wrapped themselves in their blankets and threw themselves on the ground to find repose after their long and rapid march. It was not until 8 o'clock the next morning that we received our rations of raw meat and crackers. So hungry were we that we devoured our crackers before we had cooked our meat.

Several causes are assigned for Meade's failing to fight Gen. Lee and his rapid flight across the Rapidan. One is that the roads were in such a bad condition that he had the greatest difficulty in passing his supply trains over them; another is that his men positively refused to storm our works, which they rightly deemed impregnable. In my opinion, neither of these is the true cause. Meade evidently thought that his movement upon Lee's rear would force our General to abandon his strong position on the Rapidan and fall back to Gordonsville, or perhaps to Richmond. Instead of doing this the Confederate General marched twelve miles to meet him and give him battle. This proceeding, so contrary to what he had expected, surprised Meade and made him think that his antagonist's force was much greater than had been represented to him—hence his hesitation to attack, thereby affording the Confederates opportunity & time to strongly entrench themselves. After remaining before our works for five days the Yankee commander became convinced of the folly of attempting their capture and fled precipatably across the Rapidan to his old camping ground near Culpepper.[25] The Yankee military critics, on writing of this fruitless movement, declared that Meade had been greatly surprised to find our force so strong; he having given credence to a silly but generally disseminated report that Lee's Army had been weakened by the loss of 10,000 men, who had recently been sent to re-inforce [Braxton] Bragg in Tennessee. It is well to remark here that our Army consisted of only two Corps, Ewell's & Hill's, Longstreet's Corps not being in Virginia at

25. Finding Lee's entrenchments too strong to assault, Meade decided to withdraw before winter rains made all movement impossible. Foote, *Civil War*, II, 876–77.

the time—and that the Yankee army was *at least* three times stronger than that of [the Army of] Northern Virginia.[26]

The weather was intensely cold and both armies suffered severely; in fact some of the Yankee pickets who were obliged to ford Mine Run to reach their posts were found frozen to death after the retreat of Meade.

This little affair of Mine Run was not entirely barren of results favorable to us. The victory of Johnson's Division over French's largely superior force was a brilliant little episode;[27] while [Thomas Lafayette] Rosser's Cavalry destroyed the entire amunition trains of two Yankee Corps, capturing about one hundred prisoners, forty ambulances and several hundred mules and horses. The same General also surprised a Cavalry camp, taking many prisoners and horses, and [John] Mosby the same in the vicinity of Culpepper C[ourt] H[ouse].[28]

On the 30th of November, while we were in line of battle at Mine Run, I had a most unpleasant duty to perform, viz.—the execution of Private John Connolly, of the 6th La. Regiment, a man who had deserted more than a year previously, had joined the Yankee Army—was captured at Bristow Station by a detachment from his old Regiment, tried by Court Martial, found guilty and sentenced to "be shot with musketry." He was about twenty years old and had formerly been a newsboy in New Orleans—a sullen, cross, ugly fellow, who seemed to be entirely devoid of pride or sensibility. In my official capacity as Asst. Adj. General I had to direct & superintend the execution, and a more unpleasant and revolting duty it had never been my misfortune to discharge. The orders came from Division Head Quarters in the morning and soon after the prisoner arrived at our lines, securely manacled and guarded. I sent to the Field Hospital for a Catholic Priest, who arrived at 4 o'clock in the afternoon and administered spiritual consolation to the culprit. Half an hour

26. During the Mine Run Campaign, Lee's 48,586 men faced 84,274 Yankees. *Ibid.*, 873.

27. The Battle of Payne's Farm was not the "brilliant" Confederate victory Seymour claims. Although Johnson did save the wagon train from capture, he was unable to dislodge the Yankees and withdrew during the night, leaving the field to the enemy. *OR,* Vol. XXIX, Pt. I, 846–49.

28. Rosser's cavalry attacked the wagon train of the Union I and V Corps. Rosser reported that he destroyed thirty-five to forty wagons and captured eight wagons, seven ambulances, 230 mules and horses, and ninety-five prisoners. He lost two dead and three wounded. *Ibid.*, 903–904.

later I ordered the Brigade to form on the breastworks, officers & men with only their side arms. A grave was dug fifty paces in advance of the centre of our Brigade line, at the head of which the prisoner was placed, his shackles having been removed and his arms pinnoned behind his back. Ten paces in front and facing him stood the firing party, consisting of twelve men of the company to which he had belonged. The Priest was by his side, talking to him & uttering prayers, at the same time holding before the prisoner a small crucifix of our Savior, which he kissed several times. After the good Priest had concluded the duties of his holy office, I read to the prisoner the charges against him, the findings of the Court Martial and the sentence of death. Connolly, apparently unmoved, listened attentively & after I had finished said that he had never pulled a trigger against his old comrades and that notwithstanding he had joined the Federal Army, he had resolved never to do so. He then remarked that he had no hard feelings against me for the part I was taking in his execution, for he was fully aware that I was but discharging my duty. After telling the men that it would be an act of mercy to the prisoner to take sure aim & kill him immediately, I ordered the officer commanding the firing party to proceed with the execution. The word of command was given, the muskets leveled, a similtaneous discharge followed and the vital spark fled forever from the body of John Connolly. Nine balls pierced his head and one his heart, and his death was instantanous. I hope that I may never witness a like scene again.[29]

December 3d. Our Brigade marched back to the Rapidan, resuming our old position at Raccoon Ford. The weather is bitter cold and our poor fellows, standing picket on the high, bleak banks of the River, suffer terribly from want of sufficient clothing. In our Brigade *there are two hundred and fifty men who have neither blankets nor overcoats.* It is a great wonder that these men do not freeze to death these terribly cold nights. Many of them use pine leaves and boughs wherewith to shield them from the cold, while others sit up by the

29. Although Seymour's vivid description of this execution identifies the deserter as John Connolly, the muster roll for the 6th Louisiana gives his name as Cain Comfort. Oddly, other military records indicate that both Connolly and Comfort survived the war. Booth, comp., *Records of Louisiana Confederate Soldiers,* II, 401, 414; Bound Volume 6 in Association of the Army of Northern Virginia Papers, Louisiana Historical Association Collection, Tulane University, New Orleans.

fires all night and, borrowing the blankets of their more fortunate comrades, sleep during the day. It is genuine patriotism that make men endure such privations and hardships with scarcely a murmer—and that too when they could so easily desert to the Yankee Army, where they would be comfortably clad and supplied with an abundance of food.

Speaking of patriotism puts me in mind of a little incident that showd the stuff of which the Confederate Army is made. Last Spring when we were incamped on the Rappannock, near Fredericksburg, our pickets held one bank of the River while the enemy's were on the other; there was no firing between them and they got to be on quite intimate terms with each other—exchanging friendly salutations and courtesies, and oftentimes swimming the River to hold little sociable confabs, though this last was in violation of orders. On one occasion, one of our pickets, a private of the 6th Regiment—he was off duty at the time—who was a Northerner by birth & had not been at the South for more than two years prior to the commencement of the war, discovered that a company of Yankee pickets just opposite his post were from his native city, Albany, N.Y., and that several of them were old friends and acquaintances. They invited him to a closer interview, so over the River he went to make inquiries after his aged Father and Mother, from whom he had not heard since the war began. The Yankee Captain and his men used their utmost powers of persuasion to induce their visitor to desert from the Confederate Army, promising him a safe conduct to his Parents in Albany and that he should never be called on to do duty in the Federal Army; at the same time reminding him of his tattered clothing, scanty and indifferent food. They spoke of the extreme privation & sufferings of a Confederate soldier and presented to him, in vivid contrast, the superior comforts and advantages of a Federal soldier. The ragged, half starved "Rebel" drew himself proudly up, his eye flashing and face all aglow with patriotic fervor, and contemptuously spurned the dishonorable offer. He told his tempters that he had oftentimes braved danger and death side by side with those dirty, ragged "rebs" over the River, had shared with them the exposure and sufferings of the march and the privations of the Camp—was fully aware of the superior condition of the Federal troops, but that he would not desert his colors for all the gold that the Federal Government could command. He declared that he had embarked in what he considered a righteous cause and, if it should be the will of God, he would die fighting for it. The man who made this noble reply is now with the Brigade and has neither blanket nor overcoat to shield him from the sharp, cutting winds that assail him as he performs his tour of picket duty in this bleak December weather.

When this war is closed and the historian places it's scenes and incidents on record, it will be a glorious page for admiring nations to read and ponder over; it will present thousands of instances, like the one given above, of self-sacrificing devotion—of noble, exalted, god-like heroism that fired the hearts and nerved the arms of the Confederate soldier. It will shine the brighter when placed side by side and contrasted with the foul, black, damning page of Yankee outrage, cruelty and oppression.

December 24th. The Brigade moved three *miles* back from the River to go into Camp and the men went to work, for the second time this winter, to erect huts for winter quarters. We still kept up a strong picket—one third of the Brigade at a time—at the Ford. In this camp we remained until the 4th of May, 1864; nothing occurring worthy of mention.

On this Christmas Eve our Head Quarters were in an old dilapidated negro cabin belonging to and near the residence of Mr. Eliason[30]—a quarter of a mile from Raccoon Ford. The Commander of the Brigade, Col. Monaghan of the 6th [La. Regt.], had gone over to Division Head Quarters to assist Gen. Hays, who had temporarily succeeded to Gen. Early in command of the Division, in duly observing the memorable Eve that preceeded the anniversary of the natal day of our Savior—leaving Major New, our Inspector Genl., and myself "at home" to bewail our less fortunate lot. The night was excessively cold and we passed the evening in toasting our toes before a roaring fire—talking of home & the dear ones there in anything but a joyous strain, now and then by way of parenthesis, stopping to anathematize a sable son of Africa whom we had sent to

30. The owner of this cabin was probably William P. Eliason (1807–70). He married into the Pannill family, which had several houses near the ford, and he is the only Eliason buried in the local Pannill Cemetery. Margaret C. Klein, *Tombstone Inscriptions of Orange County, Virginia* (Baltimore, 1972), 80.

Lynchburg after a demijohn of whiskey; but who, much to our annoyance, had not yet made his appearance. We had made up our mind to go egg-noggless to bed, when—about 11 o'clock—the welcome sound of horses hoofs on the crisp snow outside attracted our attention; out we rushed & there we found the tardy "Mose" with his well filled demijohn. The eggs were quickly beaten—the sugar stirred in and then the whiskey added, and we had one of the most delicious noggs that ever mortal man quaffed. Taking a couple of glasses apiece, we retired merrily to bed—to forget the hardships of a soldier's life, and dream of a joyful reunion with the dear absent ones far away in Southland.

On the 27th of December I received a leave of absence for thirty days, which I passed in the company of my Wife and child, in Augusta, Georgia—returning to camp on the 27th of January.[31]

31. The Seymour genealogical sheet in the Seymour Papers at the University of Michigan does not list a child being born in 1862 or 1863. It does give the name of one child as Eliz. Bertram but indicates only that she died in infancy. There are also two other children, named Caroline Eulalia and Elliott, but the only information given for them is that they died after 1932. The child Seymour mentions could be any of these.

THE CAMPAIGN OF 1864

SEYMOUR'S short leave must have been a welcome respite from the arduous autumn campaign. When he returned to the brigade in January, 1864, Seymour found the men suffering greatly from a lack of supplies. More than two hundred soldiers were without blankets, and many others were barefoot; all were ragged and hungry. Eventually a levy was placed on local civilians to provide Hays's men with coats and blankets. This brightened spirits, as did various forms of entertainment such as snowball battles with other units. The brigade also built a wooden theater and put on skits and plays that became popular with officers and men alike. Thus Hays's brigade coped with its situation and whiled away time in its cold winter camp along the Rapidan.[1]

In March, 1864, major changes were being made in the enemy's camp. Ulysses S. Grant, hero of Vicksburg and Chattanooga, was brought to Washington and promoted to lieutenant general. Given command of all the Union armies, Grant finalized ambitious plans to hit the Confederates on all fronts that spring. Realizing that Lee's army constituted his greatest threat, Grant decided to direct the Army of the Potomac personally in the coming campaign.[2]

GEN. U. S. Grant, having been appointed Lieut. General of the Armies of the United States, assumed the direct command of the "Army of the Potomac." To guard against any movement that Grant might make against him, Gen. Lee had caused new and stronger works to be constructed on the line of the Rapidan; and, in case the enemy should try to turn his left flank, in the direction of Madison C[ourt] H[ouse]

---

1. Jones, *Lee's Tigers*, 190–94.
2. Foote, *Civil War*, III, 3–8.

or Starmardsville, military roads had been cut and fortifications thrown up in every important position. In the latter part of March, Gen. Lee ordered Gen. M[artin] L[uther] Smith, his Chief of Engineers, to stop work on the Rapidan and to proceed to a designated point on Wilderness Run—to cut two roads running parallel to each other, thence to a point on the Catharpin Road, six miles West of Spottsylvania C[ourt] H[ouse]; thence to Hanover Junction, bridging the North and South Anna Rivers. The ordering of these roads six weeks before the campaign opened shows conclusively that Gen. Lee, at that early day, had penetrated the designs of Grant; for over those identical roads our army and wagon trains passed in the month of May. Without them the movements of the Army would have been greatly retarded and, perhaps, Gen. Lee would have been unable to prevent Grant from getting between him and Richmond.[3]

In the latter part of April, Grant's plans became manifest. [Benjamin] Butler, with two Corps, was at Fortress Monroe with the design of advancing against Petersburg; [Franz] Sigel, [who] had a force of 18,000 men at Harper's Ferry & Martinsburg, intended to sweep through the Valley of the Shenandoah, capture Staunton and Lynchburg, and cut Gen. Lee's communications with the South whence he drew all his supplies; while Grant himself, with an army greatly augmented by the accession of reserves, marines & heavy artillerists from Washington, New York, Boston, Portland and other garrisoned towns in Yankeeland, was to fall upon Lee. Burnside had joined Grant and their united forces amounted to 179,000, while the Army of Gen. Lee numbered 58,000![4]

The Army of Northern Virginia was disposed as follows: Ewell's Corps occupied the right, extending from a point three miles below Raccoon Ford nearly to Orange C[ourt] H[ouse]; Hill's Corps stretched beyond Orange C[ourt] H[ouse] for five miles; while Longstreet's Corps occupied the country immediately around Gor-

3. Seymour overstates Lee's knowledge of federal plans in the spring of 1864. It was not until mid-April that intelligence indicated that the Yankees planned a three-pronged attack across the Rapidan, through the Shenandoah Valley, and up the James River. Sources show that Lee was not certain Grant would cross the Rapidan on his right until about May 1. *Ibid.,* 120–22, 144.

4. Grant had approximately 120,000 men with the Army of the Potomac, while Sigel had 26,000 and Butler 35,000. Lee's army numbered about 60,000. *Ibid.,* 18–19; Faust, *Encyclopedia of the Civil War,* 551.

donsville—our whole line being thirty-five miles in length.

On the 3d of May the Federal Army left it's catonments around Culpepper and marched, in two columns, in the direction of Germania and Ely's Fords.

4th of May. Intelligence having been received that the Federals had commenced to cross the Rapidan, our whole army was put in motion to meet them, Gen. Lee's design being to strike Grant at or near Wilderness Church—the junction of the Germania and Fredericksburg plank road with the Orange & Fredericksburg road. Ewell's Corps took the turnpike which passed through Vediersville and Locust Grove; Hill's Corps marched over the Orange & Fredericksburg Plank Road, while Longstreet's proceeded from Gordonsville to the Catharpin Road, with the intention of marching up that road for a sufficient distance to fall upon Grant's left flank.[5]

Our Brigade broke camp at 10 a.m. and marched in the direction of Morton's Ford; but before proceeding two miles, we were ordered to retrace our steps and take the road to Mine Run. Encamped at night near Locust Grove.

May 5th. Resumed the march a short time after daylight, Johnson's & Rode's Divisions being in front of us. Early in the morning, Johnson came up with the enemy near Wilderness Run, at the junction of the Germania Road with the turnpike along which we were marching. "Old Club Foot,"[6] as Johnson was called by his men, formed his Division near Wilderness Run, his line consisting of Stafford's,[7] [J. M.] Jones' & [George H.] Steuart's Brigades, with Walker's Stonewall Brigade on the left—having been formed at right angles with the general line in order to guard against a flank attack. A few moments after this disposition had been made, the enemy made a furious assault, with four lines of battle, upon Johnson's

---

5. Grant was moving generally south past Lee's right flank. Lee was shifting his army eastward along parallel roads to intercept Grant in the Wilderness—an area of thick second-growth timber that would partly offset Grant's superior numbers and artillery. Foote, *Civil War,* III, 154; Faust, *Encyclopedia of the Civil War,* 825–27.

6. Johnson had suffered a severe foot wound earlier in the war, which did not heal well and left him somewhat handicapped—thus his nickname, "Club Foot." Faust, *Encyclopedia of the Civil War,* 397.

7. Leroy A. Stafford, former colonel of the 9th Louisiana, had been promoted to brigadier general and given command of the 2nd Louisiana Brigade in Johnson's division. For a detailed history of the 2nd Louisiana Brigade, see Jones, *Lee's Tigers.*

front; all the Brigades resisted the attack successfully except Jones's, which extended across the turnpike. Most of this Brigade broke and run in the greatest confusion, and the Yankees rushed in the breach thus made, cutting the Division in two. In vain did Gen. J. M. Jones (one of the best and bravest officers in the Army) strive to rally his demoralized troops; he and his gallant Adjutant General, Capt. [Robert D.] Early, were killed in the attempt.

At this critical juncture, Early's Division came up; our Brigade was formed on the left of the road and Gordon's on the right. At this time Jones's Virginians were running from the field thoroughly panic-stricken and the danger was great that our whole Corps would be borne back by the heavy masses of Yankees that were advancing, elated by their recent success. But Gen. Gordon, in command of his own & [Junius] Daniels's North Carolina Brigade, was ordered to advance and drive the enemy from the position they had gained between the two wings of Johnson's Division; and gallantly and successfully did he perform the work marked out for him. He drove the Yankees beyond their original position, killing & wounding a large number [and] capturing many prisoners, among which was an entire regiment that surrendered to Col. [John Hill] Lamar, of the 60th [61st] Ga. After driving the enemy for more than a mile, Gordon perceived that he was on a line with the Yankee line of battle; he quickly divided his force and changing front to the right and left struck the flanks of the enemy with great force and impetuosity, doubling up their lines and cleaning the field of Yankees for the breadth of a mile. A few minutes after the charge a field of dry sedge, over which Gordon passed and which was covered with the dead and wounded Federals, caught fire and many of the wounded perished in the flames. This splendid achievement of Gordon's forced the Federal General to withdraw his whole line to reform it and relieved Johnson's front from the great pressure which threatened to break it unretrievably.[8]

8. The Union force that so viciously crushed Jones's brigade was Gouverneur K. Warren's V Corps. Gordon's forceful counterattack relieved the threat to Ewell's line, but Seymour exaggerates his success. Ewell was under orders to avoid a general battle until Longstreet arrived on the field. Thus Gordon disengaged and pulled back to his line after pushing the Yankees back. He did not roll up the entire Union line as described by Seymour. Clifford Dowdey, *Lee's Last Campaign: The Story of Lee and His Men Against Grant—1864* (Boston, 1960), 92–99; Foote, *Civil War,* III, 155–56.

In the meantime, Stafford's Louisiana Brigade had been attacked by the enemy; but it met the charge most gallantly and hurled the attacking party back with great slaughter. But this advantage was dearly bought, for the intrepid Stafford was shot down while cheering on his men and died three days after of his wound. Brig. Gen. Leroy A. Stafford had formerly commanded the 9th La. Regiment of Hay's Brigade, and I knew him to be a most genial, wholesouled gentleman, and a cool, judicious, and at the same time, a fearless, dashing soldier. In Gen. Lee's telegraphic announcement to the War Department of the battle, our great leader paid a graceful tribute to the memory of the lamented Stafford.[9]

Soon after, Gen. Sedgwick, who commanded the Yankee [VI] Corps in our front, made an effort to turn the left flank of Ewell's Corps, which, if successful, would involve the loss of our artillery and ordnance train. Our Brigade was ordered to go, at a double quick, to the extreme left to stop this threatened movement. On our way thither, we passed poor Stafford, lying under a tree on the side of the road and suffering terribly from his wound. To those who stopped to express their sympathy, he spoke encouragingly, urging them to fight the enemy to the last and expressing a perfect willingness to yield up his life for the glorious cause in which he had so long borne arms.

We were formed on the left of Walker's Brigade, with which we were ordered to charge as quickly as possible. I was sent by Gen. Hays to Gen. Walker to acquaint him with these orders and he promised to accompany us; but, for some unexplained reason, he failed to do so. For half a mile we advanced through a thick woods, driving the Yankees easily before us; we then emerged into an open field and there we could see that the Federals outflanked us by the breadth of an entire brigade. Notwithstanding the danger of attacking such an extended line, our men were too eager and impetuous to be halted. [O]ver the field they rushed and a sharp fight ensued

9. Stafford had led his brigade toward the enemy and was forcing them back. But then the Yankees began surrounding his brigade and he ordered a retreat. Stafford was shot through the spine and mortally wounded as he oversaw the withdrawal. His death "cast a gloom over the city" of Richmond, and President Davis attended his funeral. In his telegram, Lee wrote that Stafford was mortally wounded "while leading his command with conspicuous valor." Jones, *Lee's Tigers*, 196–97; *OR*, Vol. XXXVI, Pt. I, 1028.

with a force lying in a dense pine thicket on the other side. It soon became apparent that the enemy were rapidly closing in upon both of our flanks, with the intention of enveloping our Brigade; in consequence of this, Gen. Hays was forced to withdraw his command across the field, under a murderous fire, to within a short distance of our original line. The Brigade lost heavily in this engagement—it's casualties amounted to 254, more than one third of its strength.[10]

Though we were driven back, this charge had the desired effect of staying the progress of Sedgwick's flanking movement. Among the killed was the gallant Capt. [Thomas H.] Biscoe, of the 5th Regt., my most intimate friend.[11] The following little obituary notice, written by me, was published in the Richmond *Examiner:*

In Memoriam

Killed in action on the 5th of May, 1864, at the Battle of the Wilderness, Capt. Thomas Hunt Biscoe, acting Major of the 5th La. Regt., Hays' Brigade. He was a native of New Orleans and was 23 years of age when he fell, fighting at the head of his Regiment and in the fore front of the battle. The subject of this notice was a young man of no ordinary characteristics of mind and heart. Educated at the University of Virginia, where he graduated with distinguished honors, he possessed talents and acquirements unusually extensive and brilliant for a man of his age. His character was remarkable for it's integrity and dignity; his morality was pure and elevated, unsullied by worldly temptations and the seductive influences of a soldier's life; his manners were simple, frank and winning, and his heart was filled with a warm, genial, glowing sympathy that won the love of all who enjoyed the privilege of his friendship and association. As a soldier, Capt. Biscoe's record is like his own good blade, spotless and bright; scrupulous, exact and intelligent in the discharge of his duties, he elicited the highest encomiums from his commanding officers; while his treatment of those under him was so kind and equitable as to win their utmost confidence and affections. In battle he was cool, brave and dashing—always among the foremost in the fray and the last in the retreat. There are many in Virginia and elsewhere who will mingle their tears with those of his devoted Mother over the sad fate of her noble son; the memory of his manly virtues will long occupy a prominent niche in their hearts when, "The war drums throb no longer, and the battle flags are furled."

10. No battle report was submitted for Hays's brigade so Seymour's account is the only known source for its casualties in the Battle of the Wilderness.

11. Before his death, Biscoe had been wounded and captured in two previous battles. Booth, comp., *Records of Louisiana Confederate Soldiers,* I, 194.

At 2 o'clock in the afternoon (of the 5th) the enemy made a very heavy attack upon Hill's Corps, but failed to make an impression upon it. They strove hard to force back Hill's right wing, in order to take possession of the intersection of the plank road from Germania Ford with that from Orange Court House, which, once in their occupation, would give them a favorable line for advance Southward towards Richmond. But the Divisions of Heth and [Cadmus] Wilcox stood firm as a rock and, notwithstanding the numerical superiority of the foe, handsomely repulsed his successive charges; when night came on and put a stop to the fighting in that part of the field, the Federals had not gained one inch of ground.[12]

At 8 o'clock that night, the Yankees, in five lines of battle (we afterwards learned from prisoners), made a most pertinacious and desperate effort to drive [John] Pegram's Brigade—immediately on the left of our Brigade—from it's works. Again and again did they advance until they got to within a few paces of the breastworks, and as often were they driven back with terrible slaughter, until at half past 9 o'clock they were forced to abandon the attempt. The 6th La. Regiment, on the left of our Brigade, gave great assistance to Pegram in repelling this assault by a left oblique fire which they poured into the thick Yankee columns as they advanced. The losses of the enemy were frightful and when day dawned next morning the ground was found to be literally covered with dead bodies. This closed the fighting on the 5th and General Lee had the strongest reasons for being encouraged and satisfied with his day's work. With two Corps—Longstreet not having come up—he had maintained his ground against the furious and repeated assaults of the whole of Grant's Army.

During the remainder of the night a desultory picket firing was kept up along the whole line.

May 6th. At 8 A.M. the enemy made another assault upon Pegram's works, but were driven back after half an hour's hard fighting. In this fight the gallant Pegram was severely wounded in the

---

12. A. P. Hill's Corps was a couple of miles to Ewell's right forming on the Orange Plank Road. Hit hard by Winfield Scott Hancock's II Corps, Hill was battered but managed to hold his position. Lee's situation was precarious because he was facing Grant's entire army and Longstreet's corps had not yet arrived on the field. Foote, *Civil War*, III, 162–63.

arm,[13] and the command of his Brigade devolved on Col. [John S.] Hoffman. During the remainder of the day the Yankees did not make any further attempt upon our part of the line, though heavy skirmishing was kept up, without intermission, until night fall.

On the right (Hill's Corps) a sanguinary struggle commenced a little after daylight; the enemy again striving, by the weight of his heavy columns, to break through the two Divisions of that Corps, Heth's & Wilcox's. Anderson's Division, having been left behind to guard the fords on the Rapidan, had not yet arrived on the ground. For three quarters of an hour this small force held it's ground with unflinching courage and obstinacy against at least ten times it's number; but at last, were compelled to break and fall back. At first the retreat was deliberate and orderly, but the Yankees quickly reformed and followed up their advantage with great rapidity, pushing Hill's men so hard that they fled confusedly for more than a mile. They charged to within two hundred yards of our Artillery (which could not be brought into action owing to the density of the woods) and the ordnance trains, and the total destruction, or dispersion, of Hill's Corps seemed inevitable. But, fortunately, just at this moment the head of Longstreet's Corps came upon the field and turned the tide of battle. Gen. Lee had recalled Longstreet from his flank movement up the Catharpin Road, to the relief of Hill's hard pressed troops. First came McLaw's Division, under Gen. [Joseph B.] Kershaw, which, forming at a double quick and under a most galling fire, checked the further advance of the enemy. Then [Charles W.] Field's Division arrived, then Anderson's; these on the right and left of Kershaw, the whole line went forward with a cheer that made the welkins ring. So impetuous was this charge that Longstreet's men not only regained all the ground that Hill had lost, but drove the Yankees beyond the position they had held on the previous night. The three Brigades of Field's Division that had been sent to the right of the Plank Road did not at first meet with equal success, owing to the great superiority of the enemy in numbers and position; but reinforcements coming up, the attack was renewed when the Yankees recoiled from the shock and fled the field precipitately. Thus the

---

13. Pegram was actually wounded in the leg during the May 5 attack on his brigade. Jubal Anderson Early, *A Memoir of the Last Year of the War for Independence . . . in the Year 1864 and 1865* (Lynchburg, 1867), 16–20.

symetry of our line was restored and the prospects looked bright again. Hill's scattered troops were soon collected and formed, and that Corps took position on the right of Longstreet's.

A little incident of this day's fighting is worth mentioning. When Field's men were driven back on the right of the plank road, and Longstreet's right was in great danger of being turned, Gen. Lee rode to that part of the field and placing himself at the head of [John] Gregg's (forming [John Bell] Hood's) Texas Brigade, called upon it to follow him in a charge. The Texans, anxious for the safety of their beloved and venerated Chief, refused to follow him; but declared that if he went back they would go forward. Gen. Longstreet added his own remonstrances to those of Gregg's men, and Gen. Lee withdrew. And well did the gallant Texans redeem their promise on that day, for they made one of those daring, desperate & successful charges for which they had become so famous.[14]

On this day a lamentable accident occurred, which occasioned the death of one of the best officers in the army and the wounding of the "Old War Horse," as Gen. Lee admiringly called Longstreet. When the old 1st Corps had retrieved the fortunes of the day and were driving the enemy before them, Gen. Longstreet, accompanied by his senior Major General, [Micah] Jenkins, and his own Staff, rode out on the plank road to direct the movements of a flanking column that he had sent to the right of that road to strike the flank of the enemy while they were heavily pressed in front. Unfortunately one of these Brigades, seeing this cavalcade of horsemen riding swiftly down the road, mistook them for Yankee cavalry and fired a volley at them. Poor Jenkins fell dead and Longstreet was severely wounded, a ball passing through his neck and coming out of his shoulder. Had it not been for this sad and untoward *contretemps,* a movement would have been executed which, it is believed, would have resulted in a most disastrous defeat to the Federals. As it was, before Anderson, the next in rank, could come up and assume command of the Corps, the favorable moment for the execution of Lon[g]street's plan had passed away.[15]

14. This famous incident involving Lee and the Texans actually took place earlier than Seymour states. It happened when Longstreet first arrived on the field, just as Hill's Corps was falling back, not after he had deployed Field's division. Foote, *Civil War,* III, 169.

15. After stemming the federal onslaught up the Orange Plank Road, Longstreet unleashed a crushing attack that sent Grant's left flank reeling. It was while reconnoitering to

On the left of our Corps—and consequently on the extreme left of the Army—Gen. Gordon was posted with his large Brigade of Georgians, his line extending beyond the enemy's right for the width of his Brigade front. Discovering this early in the morning, that dashing and enterprising officer was extremely desirous of moving out of his works and making a sudden attack upon the flank of the Yankee Army. I rode with him to Gen. Ewell's Head Quarters when he made known his plan to that officer & begged permission to make the attempt; but Gen. Ewell expressed the opinion that movement of that kind so early in the day would be unadvisable, inasmuch as Gordon would have to cross some open fields in full view of the enemy and thereby the smallness of his force would become apparent. He ordered Gen. Gordon [to] wait until late in the afternoon.[16]

As the sun was setting that evening, Gordon, having formed his Brigade in front of and at right angles with his works, with Pegram's Virginians on his right and [Robert D.] Johnston's North Carolinians in the rear as a supporting force, moved rapidly forward upon the enemy's flank. So sudden and impetuous was this charge that the enemy were taken completely by surprise; brigade after brigade left their works and fled from the field in terror and dismay. In vain did the Yankee commanders endeavor to change

---

continue the attack that he and Brigadier General (not Major General) Jenkins were tragically fired upon by William Mahone's brigade. *Ibid.,* 175–78; Warner, *Generals in Gray,* 155.

16. Seymour's firsthand account of Ewell's reaction to Gordon's plan further muddies an already murky incident. Early claimed that Gordon presented the plan to him that morning but was refused because there were rumors of a planned Union flanking maneuver and Burnside's corps was reported in the area Gordon proposed to attack. Ewell supported this decision, Early claimed. But Early said that these threats were gone by late afternoon, and Gordon was then given permission to launch his attack.

Ewell claimed that when Early recommended against Gordon's plan, he personally rode out to check on the situation. By the time Ewell satisfied himself that Gordon's proposal was sound and gave his permission, it was late in the afternoon.

Still other sources state that Early and Ewell simply turned down Gordon that morning. But in the afternoon Lee arrived on the scene to ask Ewell to make a diversion to relieve the pressure from Hill's and Longstreet's front. Ewell and Early were said to have demurred, but then Gordon told Lee of his plan and Lee gave him permission to attack.

Seymour, who apparently was with Gordon when he first told Ewell of his plan, gives an entirely different account of why Gordon's attack did not develop until late afternoon. One troubling question raised by Seymour's account is why, if Gordon had to cross open fields in view of the Yankees to get into position, Ewell believed waiting until late afternoon would diminish the prospect of his small force being seen by the enemy. *OR,* Vol. XXXVI, Pt. I, 1071; Early, *Memoir of the Last Year of the War,* 16–20; Freeman, *R. E. Lee,* III, 285–97.

front to receive this attack; Gordon was so quick that he gave them no time to effect this change. The slaughter of the enemy was terrible, while our loss was extraordinarily small. Onward, for a distance of a mile, Gordon pressed, sweeping everything from before him, until the darkness of night put a stop to further pursuit. Had there been one hour more of daylight Gordon would have routed the whole right wing of the Federal Army. However, the movement was a brilliant success; seven hundred prisoners were taken, among whom were Generals [Truman] Seymour and [Alexander] Shaler, and four hundred dead Federals were buried on the field next morning. Federal accounts afterwards reported that the whole of the Sixth Corps, nearly 30,000 strong, was thoroughly panic-stricken and stampeded; all this disturbance and dismay was produced by less than 5,000 "ragged rebs." Gordon was made a Major General as a reward for the gallantry and skill displayed by him on this affair.[17]

Though our skirmish line was hotly engaged, our Brigade proper took no part in this action; the enemy's balls fell as thick as hailstones in and around our works. The captured Gen. Seymour was a U.S. Regular and was in Fort Sumpter when that fortress was surrendered by Maj. Robt. Anderson to Gen. [P. G. T.] Beauregard; he had been very kind and attentive to several of the officers of our Brigade who had been wounded and left on the field at the battle of Sharpsburg, and they expressed the wish that he should be kindly treated now that he had fallen into our hands. I spoke to Col. [A. Smead] Smeds, of Gen. Ewell's Staff, on the subject and that officer extended to the captive General every courtesy within his power.

Our loss during the two days fighting in the dark, gloomy "Wilderness" was estimated, for the whole Army, at 6,000; while that of of [sic] the enemy, according to their own authorities, was 25,000! Meade's official report of the casualties in the "Army of the Potomac" gave the grand total as 23,967—this did not include those of Burnside's Corps which would increase that number by at least

17. Gordon's attack was a brilliant maneuver and marked his rise to major general. The surprise was complete, and one whole division of the VI Corps was routed (though not, as Seymour claims, the entire corps). The cost to Gordon was only about fifty men. *OR*, Vol. XXXVI, Pt. I, 1077–78; Edward Steere, *The Wilderness Campaign* (New York, 1960), 431–35.

5,000—making an aggregate of 28,967.[18] This great difference in the losses of the two armies is attributable to the fact that the Confederates, for the most part, fought behind fortifications and with a single line of battle, while the enemy marched up to the attack with five and sometimes with seven lines of battle; his solid columns offering a sure mark for our deadly rifles. In front of Ewell's Corps alone, *2,100* dead Yankees were interred by our Pioneer Corps.

May 7th. Remained in the trenches until 10 A.M. when our Brigade & that of Pegram moved to the right and front, for about three hundred yards, and took position on the Germania Road—from which the Yankees had been driven—at right angles with our works. Here we remained until night without firing a shot.

During the forenoon a large number of wounded Yankees were collected from the ground fought over on the previous night and placed in rows before our Brigade, for the examination and attention of our Surgeons. A ghastly exhibition of torn and mutilated humanity it was. Those who could bear transportation were carried in ambulances to the Field Hospitals, while those poor fellows whose wounds were so severe as to preclude removal were left to die on the ground where they were laid—a Surgeon remaining with them with instructions to do everything within his power to ameliorate their sufferings. All of these men were mortally wounded and died during the day. The last to go to the shades of another world was a brawny, good-looking, light-complexioned German, evidently fresh from his home beyond the seas. He could not speak a word of English and at first seemed much frightened, no doubt thinking that he had fallen into the hands of the Philistines; but in a little while, when he saw how tenderly our Surgeon ministered to his relief, the expression of his countenance changed into one of grateful surprise. As evening drew on & the pallor that overspread his face and the labored breathing told that the man's hour of dissolution was near at hand, quite a crowd of soldiers gathered around him, evincing considerable interest in his fate. A tear rolled from the eye of the dying "Fed" and trickled down his cheek; a rough looking "Reb" who noticed it remarked that the man was thinking of his

18. Seymour greatly overestimated Grant's losses in the Wilderness. The approximate totals were Confederates, 7,500; Army of the Potomac, 17,500; and Burnside's corps, 1,500. Faust, *Encyclopedia of the Civil War,* 827; *OR,* Vol. XXXVI, Pt. I, 907.

vrow and little ones. A minute afterwards, when his respirations had apparently ceased, the man that made the above sympathetic remark, knelt down by the side of the dying man & thrust his hands into his pockets in quest of a knife and greenbacks, two articles very highly prized from their scarcity by the Confederate soldiers. A bystander [who] effected to be greatly shocked at this exhibition of rapacity on the part of his comrade, called out to him that the Yankee was not dead and that it was a shame to rob a dying man, declaring that the man's ghost would haunt him ever after. Thus appealed to, the would-be plunderer withdrew, leaving the contents of the Yankee's pocket undisturbed. The soldier who had appeared to be so much shocked at the attempted robbery, then approached the body, felt of the pulse, declared that the man was as dead as a "door nail," and then quietly & with the greatest *sang froid,* drew from the pockets of the dead "Fed" a well filled pocket-book and several other articles of less value—much to the chagrin of the man that had made the unsuccessful attempt at plundering, & to the great amusement of the bystanders at the cleverness of the trick. I walked away disgusted, moralizing upon "man's inhumanity to man," when war and a familiarity with it's horrors had hardened the hearts and blunted the sensibilities of those engaged in it.

Grant had been completely foiled in his attempt to get between Lee's Army and Richmond, and force the Confederate General to fight at the great disadvantage of having his communications with his base of supplies cut off. Therefore, it became necessary for Grant to change the details of his general plan and, on this day, he withdrew his army to the Wilderness & Spottsylvania Road, with the evident intention of trying the Fredericksburg route to Richmond.

The great battle of the Wilderness—the bloodiest of the war[19]— was fought almost exclusively by infantry; owing to the density of the woods, artillery could not be used and there were not more than six pieces of cannon brought into action by either side, and they were posted on the roads. Thus it was that more than three hundred of these usually loud mouthed "dogs of war" were dumb and in-

19. Actually, Gettysburg was the bloodiest battle of the Civil War, with total casualties amounting to almost fifty thousand. Faust, *Encyclopedia of the Civil War,* 307.

nocuous. But the more unerring and deadly musket plied its awful work, and heaped the field with hecatombs of dead. Never was there a more grim and ghastly spectacle of the horrors and terrible destructiveness of War than was presented under the deep and solemn shades of the Wilderness; while the atmosphere for miles around was filled with the noisome odors that came up from the putrifying corpses. In this connection, I will mention a curious fact, which I give as the result of my observation on a number of battle-fields and which I have heard substantiated by many other persons. The dead body of a Confederate soldier, when left exposed for three or four days, seems to wither away—the skin becomes shrunken and assumes a yellow, saffron color—while, strange to say, it emits little or no odor; on the contrary, the body of a dead Yankee swells up to an enormous size—turns to a dark purple color and becomes, in a very short time, exceedingly offensive to the smell. This is ascribed by many to the superior *keeping* of the Federal soldier, owing to the comparatively rich food upon which he lived.

On the evening of the 7th of May, it was observed that Grant had extended his left and that a portion of his Army was on the march to Spottsylvania C[ourt] H[ouse].[20] At dark Gen. Lee sent Longstreet's Corps, now under the command of Anderson, preceeded by a large force of Cavalry, to prevent the Federals from seizing that place and the commanding positions in the vicinity. Our Brigade moved down the line of entrenchments to the right; so slowly and cautiously was the movement conducted—there still being a large Yankee force in our front—that when day dawned we had accomplished a distance of only one mile and a half.

May 8th. At 8 A.M. the march was resumed, we passed through White Hall to the Catharpin Road, marched down that road to within a mile of Spottsylvania, when we turned off to the left and went into position on the right of Rodes' Division, in the line of Johnson's Division to which we had been, on this day, assigned—

---

20. Grant was using a maneuver he would repeat during the campaign. Failing to turn Lee's flank in the Wilderness, Grant disengaged and attempted to make another run around Lee's right flank. If the federals could seize Spotsylvania Court House, they would be between Lee and Richmond, forcing Lee to attack Grant's entrenched position. Foote, *Civil War,* III, 189.

Stafford's Brigade on our left and the remnant of Jones's on our right.[21]

The race between Anderson's Corps and the 5th Yankee Corps to get first to the Court House and take possession of the most favorable positions around that place was a very exciting and closely contested one. The Yankee General [Gouverneur K.] Warren, having the shorter road, got there first; but his advantage was but temporary, for Anderson soon after came up and, driving the enemy back for two miles, held the line that Gen. Lee had previously selected until the remainder of the Army reached the ground.[22]

May 9th. It was one o'clock in the morning before our Division reached it's allotted place in the line, where our men were hastily put to work to build fortifications. Though our supply of entrenching tools was very limited, our men toiled with such a will that by daylight we had quite a strong line of works to fight behind; these were further improved and strengthened during the day. There was heavy skirmishing during the morning on the right and the commander of the 6th Yankee Corps, Gen. Sedgwick, was killed. He was one of the best Generals in the Federal Army; our Corps had been pitted against his on several memorable occasions, at Fredericksburg, Rappahannock Station & the Wilderness, and we recognized it as the best fighting and best handled Corps in the Yankee Army. An ardent practical believer in the potency of whiskey in arousing that species of valor denominated "Dutch courage," he always plied his troops with the *spiritus frumenti* before putting them into battle. This pleasant little idiosyncracy made him very popular among his soldiers, who mourned his loss sincerely.[23]

The position held by our Division was a salient angle in the gen-

21. Because of heavy casualties in the two Louisiana brigades, they were too small for effective service after the Wilderness. As a result, Lee transferred Hays's brigade to Johnson's division and consolidated it with Stafford's brigade. Hays was named commanding officer, but the two brigades kept their separate organization. Nonetheless, the new consolidated brigade usually was referred to as Hays's brigade. Jones, *Lee's Tigers,* 201.

22. Anderson actually arrived at Spotsylvania about a minute ahead of the federal infantry and managed to hold the crossroads for Lee. Foote, *Civil War,* III, 196.

23. Sedgwick was killed by a Confederate sharpshooter after uttering his famous last words, "They couldn't hit an elephant at this distance." Seymour's attributing his soldiers' fighting ability to whiskey was a common belief Confederates held about numerous Yankee units. Warner, *Generals in Blue,* 431.

eral line of works, and our men did not like it at all; it was so liable to be enfiladed by artillery and would be a dangerous trap to be caught in should the line be broken on the right or left. Gen. M[artin] L[uther] Smith, Gen. Lee's Chief of Engineers, told me that it had not been originally designed to run the line out so far in that direction; but owing to the presence of a hill in that part of the field, upon which the enemy might place batteries and give us much trouble, this salient had to be constructed. An unfortunate work it turned out to be.[24]

May 10th. Heavy skirmishing began early in the morning in front of our Brigade and "those people," as Gen. Lee always called the Yankees, manifested a strong desire to *feel* of our line and ascertain it's strength. They soon gained the wished for information, and paid dearly for it. At 10 A.M. they marched, in beautiful line, up to the front of our works, two other lines being in the woods behind to act as a supporting force. Jumping a fence two hundred yards distant from our works, the color bearers planted their flags in a road; the blue coats rallied around them looked fierce and seemed determined to do something desperate. Their officers flourished their swords and ordered them to charge; they had not advanced ten paces before they were greeted by a withering volley from our rifles which brought them to a halt; another volley put them to the right about and made them scamper, in inglorious haste, back to their fortifications. They had felt the strength of our line and were so well satisfied that they did not attempt to gain any further information on the subject. When the Yankees fell back, a heavy line of skirmishers was thrown forward from our Brigade and a number of prisoners taken.

At 4 o'clock P.M., the enemy made a most furious assault on our right—Hill's Corps under Gen. Early[25]—coming up to the attack with seven lines of battle. The contest raged for two hours with unprecedented violence, when the enemy were forced to retire without breaking our line at any one point. *On two* occasions they came

24. This salient was dubbed the Mule Shoe by the Confederates because of the way it bulged out from the main line. It was approximately half a mile wide and one mile deep, and Lee recognized its vulnerability and began constructing a new line of defenses across its base. But this was a slow process because the woods were dense. Freeman, *R. E. Lee,* III, 311–13.

25. Early took temporary command of the III Corps after Hill became too ill to continue leading it. *Ibid.,* 304–305.

up to our breastworks and our men fought them with bayonets and clubbed muskets; but Gen. Lee had so strengthened this part of the line in anticipation of an attack, that the enemy could not break through. The slaughter among the Yankees in this desperate conflict was awful.

On the left of our Brigade—two Brigades, Stafford's and Walker's, intervening—[George] Doles' Georgia Brigade was posted. At that point the two opposing lines of battle came within two hundred yards of each other. The Yankees were in a thick woods, behind which was a valley that afforded them great facilities for secretly massing troops for a sudden attack. At 5 P.M., a dash was made at Doles' line, which, after a hard fight and gallant defence, was successful. The Yankees broke through and, getting some three hundred yards behind our works, seemed at one time to have effected a permanent lodgment there and captured a battery of the "Richmond Howitzers." The situation of our Division was extremely critical and we were entirely cut off from the remainder of the army, the enemy being in our rear. But the Yankee success was short lived. Gen. Gordon quickly formed his own and Pegram's Brigades at right angles with our line, and making a gallant charge, drove the enemy out, took many prisoners, recaptured our cannon, and restored the line to it's old formation.[26]

A few minutes after the attack made in the morning upon our Brigade, Gen. Hays was severely wounded by a stray bullet. He went to the rear to [a] Hospital and Col. Wm. Monaghan, of the 6th La. Regt., assumed command of the Brigade.[27]

May 11th. At 10 A.M. the Brigade was moved to the left, to the position from which Doles had been driven on the previous evening. This was considered the weakest portion of our works; the Yankee line ran so close up to it that it was the least desirable to

26. This temporary breakthrough was the brainchild of a young Union colonel, Emory Upton. Using twelve regiments, he attacked on a narrow front, four lines deep, without stopping to return fire. Once inside the rebel works, his men fanned out right and left and captured the works, including Captain Benjamin Smith, Jr.'s, company of the Richmond Howitzers. Grant was impressed with the assault and decided to use the same tactic with an entire corps two days later. Foote, *Civil War*, III, 207–10; Jennings Cropper Wise, *The Long Arm of Lee: The History of the Artillery of the Army of Northern Virginia* (New York, 1959), 787.

27. According to Ewell's official report, Hays was shot the preceding day. He never rejoined the brigade but was transferred to the Trans-Mississippi Department upon recovering from his wound. *OR*, Vol. XXXVI, Pt. I, 1072; Jones, *Lee's Tigers*, 208.

occupy, for the troops were kept constantly on the alert in anticipation of an attack. Our men did not like the change at all, being anxious to fight behind works of their own construction; but felt highly flattered when they heard that they had been sent there ni [sic] obediance to an order from Lt. Gen. Ewell, that the best and most reliable Brigade in the Corps should be posted at that point. In going into position we lost several men, among whom was Ensign [Arthur] Duchamp, of the 8th Regt., who had been very severely wounded at Gettysburg, had been promoted for his gallant conduct on that field, and had just returned to duty.[28] He was killed while planting his colors on the works. Young Duchamp was naturally a mild, amiable man, but in battle he was as brave as a lion, and no man carried his flag closer to the enemy than he did.

In and around the works were thickly strewned dead Yankees, guns and cast off accoutrements—mementoes of Gordon's work the day before. The enemy fired heavily upon us whenever we tried to bury their dead, so we were obliged to let them remain on the top of the ground and fester and putrify in the hot sun. Our boys collected together the guns and, loading them with slugs, placed them on top of the works, ready for use; each man had at least three guns, which would enable him to fire as many times without stopping to reload—a great desideratum where the enemy had but a short distance to charge. During the whole day we were expecting an attack, but sharp skirmishing was the only excitement we had in the fighting line.

Soon after dark, heavy columns of the enemy were discovered to be marching off to the right and taking the road to Fredericksburg. Knowing that it was all important that his army should move *pari passu* with Grant's, and believing that his antagonist was shifting his ground, Gen. Lee ordered every preparation to be made to move by daylight next morning. With this view the battalion of Artillery (19 pieces) which had been posted on the right of our old position, now occupied by Jones' Brigade, was moved back to the road to be in readiness for the march. The removal of this artillery proved to be

28. Besides being wounded at Gettysburg, Duchamp was captured both early in the war and at Rappahannock Station. Tragically, he had just been promoted from private to ensign on May 4, 1864. On his military record was written, "A brave and gallant young man." Booth, comp., *Records of Louisiana Confederate Soldiers*, II, 691.

most unfortunate. This movement of the enemy was a very clever *ruse de guerre,* which completely deceived our Generals for a time. The Yankees, it appears, moved down the Fredericksburg road— passing in front of their camp fires in plain view of our troops— until reaching a point from which they could not be seen by our videttes, they countermarched and, moving behind their fires, re- turned to the valley which I have already described as lying imme- diately behind the enemy's line that fronted our Brigade. Our men were on the *qui vive* all night and stood, with muskets in hand, ready to receive hostile visitors.

May 12th. My [32nd] birth-day, and a stirring one it was. It was nearly 3 o'clock in the morning before we could arrive at a conclu- sion as to the meaning of the Yankee movements, they seeming to be marching in every direction; at that hour it became apparent that they were massing very heavily in our immediate front. I imme- diately went to the Head Quarters of Major General Edward John- son and communicated to him this intelligence. He quickly in- formed Gen. Ewell and requested that the Artillery Battalion be sent back to it's old place on Jones's right; he also dispatched orders to his Brigade commanders to be in readiness, and that Gordon's & Pegram's Brigades should form behind our Brigade to assist it in repelling the expected assault. A few minutes before daylight, these Brigades were in the position assigned to them, and the men stood expectant and ready to do their whole duty on that day. It was the first time that our Brigade had been supported by two lines of battle, and we all felt confident of resisting any force that could be brought against us. But we were doomed to be disappointed, for the enemy, though massed in our front, did not attempt to assault our portion of the line. Just at dawn of day, there suddenly burst upon our startled ears a sound like the roaring of a tempestuous sea; the woods before us fairly rang with the hoarse shouts of thousands of men—

> "O 'twas a din to fright a monster's ear;
> To make an earthquake! sure it was the roar
> Of a whole herd of *Yankees.*"

Click, click, sounded along our ranks, as each man cocked his mus- ket and every eye was strained to discover, in the dim light of early morn, the first appearance of the Yankee line as it emerged from the woods. Some moments elapsed before we could see a single Yankee, when suddenly the enemy poured out of the woods in front of our right, and marching obliquely to the left (our right), reached the broad open field in front of Jones's Brigade. Never have I seen such an exciting spectacle as then met my gaze. As far as the eye could reach, the field was covered with the serried ranks of the enemy, marching in close columns to the attack. Thus was the time for our artillery to open, but not a shot was heard, our guns, unfortunately, not having gotten into position. The Yankees advanced with *twelve lines of battle,* and unmolested by artillery, soon reached the works behind which the remnant of Jones' Brigade, so cut up and demorialized at the Wilderness, was posted. These troops, formed in a single line and unsupported, and seeing the overwhelming force advancing against them, became panick stricken and ingloriously fled the field without firing scarcely a shot. The Yankees rushed over the works, taking Major Genl. Johnson prisoner, and capturing the Battalion of Artillery (19 guns) just arrived on the ground but not in time to unlimber and go into action. They quickly charged to the right and left, along the line of our works, taking our forces in flank and capturing the larger portion of Jones's, Steuart's, Stafford's & Walker's Brigades besides thirty-eight men from the extreme right of our Brigade who had not heard the order to withdraw. Gordon's & Pegram's Brigades were immediately marched, by the right flank, to the woods lying behind the works out of which Jones's men had been driven, and succeeded in stopping the progress of the Yankees in that direction. Our Brigade moved to the left for a distance of one hundred and fifty yards, and, changing front to the right, formed line of a battle on a small hill where was posted a battery of artillery. The enemy, greatly elated by this easy success, came sweeping down the line of our works, yelling like devils; arriving at the foot of the hill on the crest of which we were posted, they reformed and made repeated efforts to ascind, but were as often met by such a steady and murderous fire that they soon gave up the attempt and retired to the works they had captured. Had they forced us from this hill, they would have have [sic] driven a wedge between the two wings of the Army and forced Gen. Lee to retreat, which would have been attended by great loss of men and material.

A few minutes after the Yankees had broken over our works, when Gen. Gordon with his own and Pegram's Brigade was about to charge them, Gen. Lee rode out in front of the line and taking off his hat waved it in the direction of the enemy, thereby indicating his intention to lead them in the fight. The men cried out to him to come back, but the old hero moved not and seemed determined to lead the charge. As he sat there on his splendid horse, his form erect, his grey head uncovered and eyes flashing with excitement, he appeared imposing and grand, and the soldiers manifested their admiration for him by loud cheers. Gen. Gordon then rode up to him and implored him in the strongest terms to give up the idea of going into the charge. When Gen. Gordon told him that if he led his (Gordon's) men into action it would be considered by the Army as indicating a want of confidence on the part of the Commander in Chief, in the ability and courage of Gen. G[ordon], Gen. Lee moved away to another part of the field, where he and Gen. Ewell were conspicuously engaged in rallying the fugitives of Johnson's Division who had escaped capture. There was a strong contrast in the demeanor of these two Generals on this occasion. Gen. Lee was calm, collected and dignified, he quietly exhorted the men not to forget their manhood and their duty, but to return to the field and strike one more blow for the glorious cause in which they were enlisted. Gen. Ewell was greatly excited and, in a towering passion, hurled a terrible volley of oaths at the stragglers from the front, stigmatizing them as cowards, etc. It is hardly necessary to say that Gen. Lee's course was by far the more effective of the two. Ewell's profanity at this time caused a good deal of merriment after the battle. He had formerly been noted as one of the hardest swearers in the army, but having lost a leg at the second Battle of Manassas, afterwards married, joined the church, and, of course, abandoned the habit of cursing; the excitement of this occasion was too much for his religious scruples, and he swore with all of his old time vehemence and volubility.

At 7 A.M., [Stephen Dodson] Ramseur's N[orth] C[arolina] Brigade formed on our right and advanced at a charge; the steadiness with which they went forward, fighting at every step, was most admirable and elicited loud cheers from our men. At last, after two hours of hard fighting, Ramseur re-captured a portion of the works. On the extreme right of the works captured by the enemy in the morning, Pegram's Virginians had gained a foothold, having driven out the Yankees after several desperate charges. The enemy still held the *salient* between Ramseur and Pegram and against this Gen. Ewell hurled brigade after brigade; but the Yankees were so strongly posted on a thickly wooded hill that our attacking forces, one after the other, were driven back, torn and bleeding, to the inner line of fortifications. The enemy had brought to this attack three full Corps, the larger portion of his army;[29] his artillery enfiladed our line from both flanks and at the same time kept up an infernal fire upon our front.

Never before during this war had so many men fought within so contracted a space. Masses of troops were thrown again and again against Ramseur & Pegram, but at each onset those gallant Brigades sent them *reeling* back with immense slaughter. Though the flood gates of heaven opened and the rain descended for more than an hour, it did not cause the fire to slacken—the heavy thunder of the artillery and the continuous roll of the musketry rising high above the noise of the storm. Thus the battle raged fiercely for eleven long hours. At 2 P.M. the Yankees were driven out of the works, excepting a small angle of about one hundred yards in length which was still held by their sharpshooters. Disgusted and disheartened at the result of their days bloody work, which had commenced so promisingly in the morning, they ceased their attacks and passed the remainder of the day in heavy skirmishing.[30] In this day's fighting we

29. Winfield Scott Hancock's II Corps made the initial assault on the Mule Shoe, followed shortly by Wright's and Burnside's corps, which hit the western and eastern sides respectively. Foote, *Civil War*, III, 218, 220.

30. Fighting continued along parts of the line until after midnight. At that time, Lee finally gave orders for those units still holding parts of the Bloody Angle to fall back to the new line of defense built across the base of the Mule Shoe.

Seymour's account of the fight at the Bloody Angle provides important new information about what happened there. Since the two Louisiana brigades had been consolidated and placed in Johnson's division, it has generally been assumed that Hays's brigade was overrun and captured with Stafford's brigade. Even official reports fail to mention that Hays's old brigade was put further to the left at Doles's former position. Because of this, the crucial role the Louisianians played in stemming the Yankee breakthrough has been overlooked. One unpublished source supports Seymour's claim that the brigade stopped the Union advance on the

lost about three thousand prisoners—most of Johnson's Division having been taken. Our losses in killed & wounded was heavy, but not near as much so as those of the enemy.[31]

Gen. Ewell resolved to abandon the salient angle, the loss & re-capture of which had cost him so dearly; so, soon after dark, he withdrew his troops to the main line of fortifications, thereby short-ening & strengthening his line. Our Division had been so badly shattered that it was withdrawn from the front & placed in reserve for the purpose of reorganization. In this battle we lost one of the best field officers in our Brigade, Lt. Col. Bruce Menger, Comdg. the 5th La. Regt.

May 13th. The Brigade moved two miles to the rear & went into camp. No fighting along the line.

May 14th. Brigade still in reserve. In the afternoon the enemy as-saulted the right of A. P. Hill's line, but were repulsed with great loss. A portion of the attacking force was composed of negroes, who cried out as they advanced, "Remember Fort Pillow."[32] This so exasperated Wright's Georgians that jumping over their works, they drove the negroes back for a distance of half of a mile, slaughtering large numbers & capturing three stands of colors & *only seventy-nine prisoners*. This was the first occasion on which negro troops had been brought in contact with Lee's Army.[33]

May 15th. Moved to join our Division & took our position in the breastworks. Nothing of an exciting nature occurred during the day.

May 16th & 17th. In the trenches. All quiet.

May 18th. Heavy skirmishing in our front to day, which we knew to be the prelude to an advance on the part of the enemy. At 11 o'clock, a line of battle was seen crossing the open field in our front;

---

western side of the Mule Shoe. G. P. Ring, an officer in the 6th Louisiana, wrote his wife, "Genl. Ewell says our Brigade saved his left, by the determined stand we made which checked the enemy's advance. I hope he will mention it in his report." G. P. Ring to wife, May 15, 1864, in Army of Northern Virginia Papers, Part I; *OR,* Vol. XXXVI, Pt. I, 1072–73.

31. Lee lost about 6,000 men at the Mule Shoe, while Grant lost approximately 6,800. Foote, *Civil War,* III, 223.

32. On April 12, 1864, Confederate Lieutenant General Nathan Bedford Forrest assaulted and captured Fort Pillow, a Union stronghold on the Mississippi River. The fort was largely garrisoned by black troops, many of whom were killed when they tried to surrender. Faust, *Encyclopedia of the Civil War,* 277–78.

33. Brigadier General Edward Ferrero's division in Burnside's corps consisted of black troops and must have made this attack. *OR,* Vol. XXXVI, Pt. I, 207, 986.

the Yankees were permitted to get within three hundred yards, when thirty-five pieces of artillery that were posted along our Brigade front, opened upon them with grape & cannister. When the smoke lifted from the field we discovered the enemy flying in haste & disorder—his dead & wounded, strewed thickly over the field, showed the terrible execution our artillery had effected. Two other lines successfully advanced, each time being allowed to get nearer to our works when our grim "Napoleons" poured upon them a murderous storm of iron which tore great rents in their ranks & drove them crippled & shattered from the field.[34] The force that made this attack was the Irish Division, formerly commanded by Gen. [Thomas Francis] Meagher, that fought so desperately at the battle of Fredericksburg in the assault upon Marye's Heights.[35]

On this day Gen. Lee informed the army, through a Genl. Order, that on the 13th inst., Gen. [John C.] Breckenridge had defeated Gen. [Franz] Sigel near Newmarket, in the Shenandoah Valley, & had driven him across the Shenandoah. Breckenridge captured six pieces of artillery & one thousand stand of small arms, & forced Sigel to destroy the larger portion of his train. Thus an effectual estoppel was put upon the enemy's projected movement against Staunton, Lynchburg & Gen. Lee's commications with the South.[36]

May 19th. On this day Grant, having been brought to a realizing sense of the futility & folly of fighting any longer on the Spottsylvania line, began to move a portion of his army to the left, with a view of passing from the line of the river Po, down the valley of the

34. Henry Egan, of the Louisiana Brigade, claimed that when the attacks were broken up and the Yankees fled, the Louisianians jumped on top of their works, waved their slouch hats, and "called to them to come back but they had no notion of coming again." He claimed to have seen approximately 250 dead federals on the field though the Louisiana Brigade had two men wounded. Henry Egan to brother, June 21, 1864, in J. S. Egan Family Papers, Louisiana State University, Baton Rouge.

35. Seymour is referring to the Irish Brigade, a unit dominated by Irishmen from New York and Massachusetts. Originally commanded by Thomas Francis Meagher, it led the attack against Marye's Heights at Fredericksburg on December 13, 1862, and suffered heavy losses. Meagher was transferred west before this May 18, 1864, attack, but the brigade still served in the 1st Division, II Corps, of Meade's army. Faust, *Encyclopedia of the Civil War,* 384–85, 483.

36. Major General Franz Sigel, with 6,500 men, had been ordered to seize control of the Shenandoah Valley from Major General John C. Breckinridge's 5,000 rebels. On May 15, 1864, Breckinridge attacked Sigel at New Market and won a battle made famous by the participation of Virginia Military Institute cadets. As a result of this defeat, Sigel was relieved of command four days later. *Ibid.,* 537–38.

Rappahannock. In doing this he first withdrew his forces from the front of Ewell's Corps. Gen. Lee determined to retard his progress in that direction & ordered Ewell to attack him after dark upon his right flank, knowing that this would cause Grant to halt his marching columns in expectation of a general attack. Ewell marched his troops out of the works at 8 o'clock that night and made an attack upon the Yankees' right, but with no decided result other than the one Gen. Lee intended to effect. The enemy were found to be so well prepared & the night being too dark for maneuvring, Ewell, after some spirited skirmishing, withdrew his Corps back to the works. Grant, however, was induced to pause in his movement by the left flank and Lee had ample time to make his preparations to change his line to correspond with that of his antagonist.[37]

May 20th. Remained quiet all day. At night recd. orders to move at daylight next morning.

May 21st. Moved promptly at daylight & marched until 10 P.M., having made frequent halts during the day. Intelligence reached us the [sic] Grant had arrived at Bowling Green intending to march down the well known highway that leads from that place to Richmond. Gen. Lee was hastening to Hanover Junction to intercept him.

May 22nd. Started before daylight & reached Hanover Junction at 1 P.M. Pickett's & Breckenridge's Divisions arrived from Richmond. We were now behind the North Anna River & the enemy were reported advancing slowly and cautiously towards that river. The north bank of the river was so high & presented so many favorable positions for artillery, that the enemy could easily cross the river under cover of his batteries.

May 23d. Brigade moved at 1 P.M. parallel with the railroad in the direction of the River & took position in front of the [Thomas] Doswell House, some two miles below the Bridge; remained there till 8 o'clock, when we returned to the Junction where we bivoucked for the night. The enemy made his appearance on the other side of

---

37. Grant's objective in his slide to Lee's right was Hanover Junction, a rail junction on the south side of the North Anna River, about twenty miles south of Spotsylvania. During the maneuver Ewell asked for and received Lee's permission to probe Grant's right flank to gain information. In doing so, his corps was hit hard by the federals and badly trounced. Ewell was fortunate to retire from the engagement with approximately nine hundred casualties. *OR*, Vol. XXXVI, Pt. I, 1073–74; Freeman, *R. E. Lee*, III, 334–44; Foote, *Civil War*, III, 240–42, 265.

the river and opened fire with his artillery upon our small force guarding the Bridge. It was not Gen. Lee's object to offer any serious resistance to the enemy's crossing and the force at the Bridge was merely to retard their advance until our line could be formed and fortifications constructed.

May 24th. Brigade moved with the Division (Gordon's) [38] to a field in front of the junction, where we remained until 11 o'clock A.M., ready to reinforce any portion of the line that might be attacked. The enemy made several ineffectual efforts to break Hill's line on the left. At 11 o'clock our Division marched up the railroad for a couple of miles & took position to support Hill. At sun-down marched one mile below the Junction & relieved Breckenridge's Division along the line of [the] railroad.

May 25th. Engaged all day in entrenching. Enemy made an attack upon Lonstreet's [sic] line of skirmishers, but failed to drive them in.

May 26th. Gen. Smith, Chief of Engineers, not liking our position, moved our Brigade to a hill 200 yards in front of the railroad & we went to work making another line of fortifications. Heavy skirmishing in front of our left in which our sharpshooters. [sic] The enemy tried hard to dislodge our sharpshooters, bringing up a line of battle & using artillery for that purpose, but he failed to drive them away. This was one of several occasions during this campaign when our sharpshooters—all picked men—had successfully resisted the charges of lines of battle.

May 27th. This morning it was discovered that the enemy had recrossed the North Anna & was marching down that river. Grant not likeing the appearance of Gen. Lee's works in front of the junction, and not wishing to fight with an unfordable river immediately in his rear, concluded to again "change his base;" so he swung his army from the North Anna around & across the Pamunkey [River], intending to try McClelland's former "on to Richmond route." [39]

38. On May 20, Early resumed command of his division and Gordon was given a new division formed around his brigade and Johnson's old division. This new division included the Louisiana Brigade. *OR,* Vol. XXXVI, Pt. I, 1073.

39. Grant hoped to get between Lee and Richmond by again sliding around Lee's right flank—this time toward Cold Harbor. In the spring of 1862, George B. McClellan was also near Cold Harbor when he attempted to capture Richmond by moving against the city from the east up the peninsula formed by the York and James rivers. After coming within five miles

Though Grant had magnilaquently telegraphed Lincoln, during the battle of Spottsylvania, that "he proposed to fight it out on that line, if it took him all summer;" he had been so handsomely foiled in all his movements by Gen. Lee, that now, before the summer had even set in, he was forced to abandon his own "line" & attempt the one on which "Little Mac" had so signally failed.

Early in the morning our army was put in motion, our Division being in the van. Marched all day & bivouacked at night on the road between Ashland and Atlee's Station. On this day [Philip] Sheridan's Cavalry occupied Hanovertown on the Pamunkey River.

May 28th. Moved before day, crossed the railroad at Atlee's Station, & took the road to Coal Harbor. Halted at 11 o'clock A.M. near Shady Grove Church, where we remained all night & part of next day. We were now within 13 miles of Richmond. Some two miles in our front our Cavalry had a very sharp fight with [the] enemy's advance, which lasted for four hours. The stubborn resistance made at this point by two Cavalry Brigades, recently arrived from the coast of Georgia & South Carolina, to the advance of the enemy's infantry, was the theme of general admiration throughout the whole army.

Gen. Ewell being sick, Gen. Early assumed command of the 2d Corps.[40]

May 29th. Division moved at 2 o'clock P.M. to the left & front about five hundred yards & went into line of battle on the right of Field's Division, Hill's Corps. Brigade occupied the center, Gordon's old Brigade being on our left & [William] Terry's Virginia [Stonewall] Brigade on our right. Went to work putting up breastworks.

May 30th. Moved to the right with the Corps at 3 o'clock P.M. for the purpose of striking the enemy's flank. Rodes drove the enemy back for half a mile, thus getting him away from the vicinity of the Mechanicsville turnpike & forcing him to change the direction of his line of battle. Ramseur, in command of Early's Divison, following close behind Rodes, deployed into line on his left. Seeing a force

---

of the city, he was repelled by Lee during the Seven Days' Campaign. Faust, *Encyclopedia of the Civil War,* 571.

40. Ewell was suffering from a severe case of diarrhea. Although ready to resume command in a few days, he was put in command of Richmond's defenses, leaving Early to command the II Corps. *OR,* Vol. XXXVI, Pt. I, 1074.

of Yankees in front of his right, Ramseur sent forward Pegram's Brigade to charge them. It was not until they had gotten to within one hundred yards of the woods that they perceived that the Yankees were not only in overwhelming force, but that they had very strong works, hitherto masked by the thicket of dwarf pine. The gallant Brigade did not stop, however, but pushed on with a yell to the charge. Again & again did the brave Virginians advance up to the works & as often were they driven back by the pitiless storm of bullets that was hurled into their faces, until, at last, they were ordered back to the general line. The loss of this Brigade was terrible— more than half of it's numbers having been killed & wounded, including nearly all the field officers. Ramseur was much blamed for not putting his whole Division into the charge, instead of sending up one small Brigade to be cut to pieces by a largely superior force behind strong breastworks. Night coming on put a stop to the fight.[41]

The Brigade remained on the Mechanicsville Road until 9 o'clock at night, when we moved two hundred yards to the left of that road & went into line of battle.

May 31st. Engaged all the morning throwing up breastworks. At 5 o'clock in the afternoon went back to the position that we first held on the left.

June 1st. Returned to the Mechanicsville Road & was posted immediately on the right of that road. Late in the afternoon our Corps attacked the right flank of the enemy, driving the Yankees for a mile & a half & doubling up their right, [and] forced it upon their centre. Our Brigade reached the Yankee works & took possession of them, when a battery only two hundred & fifty yards distant opened a furious fire upon us. At the same time, a vacant space having been left on our right, the Yankees took advantage of it & rushed in there; this compelled us to fall back a hundred yards to prevent our flank from being turned. After dark we went to work fortifying.[42] Dur-

---

41. Using the same tactic to delay Grant's movement on May 30 as he did on May 19, Lee had the II Corps hit the enemy's right flank. But again it was a botched attack with poor execution. Although Seymour blamed Ramseur, Early was actually responsible, having failed to commit his entire corps and ordering Pegram's brigade to make its disastrous assault alone. Foote, *Civil War,* III, 278–80; Dowdey, *Lee's Last Campaign,* 279–80.

42. Seymour is obviously mistaken on the date of this action and also overstates its size and importance. The only fighting of note by Early's corps came on June 2. Early probed

ing this movement Lt. Col. [Germain A.] Lester, of the 8th La. Regt., was killed; he was a gallant soldier & a meritorious gentleman. Col. Monaghan, being sick, went to [the] Hospital in Richmond and Col. [Alcibiades] DeBlanc[43] assumed command of the Brigade.

June 2d. The enemy having disappeared from our front, the Brigade fell back to it's old fortifications & remained there all day, awaiting orders to move.

Grant had on the 1st inst., with a loss of two thousand men, possessed himself of Coal Harbor, an important stategic [sic] point, it being the point of convergence of all the roads leading to Richmond, his objective point and to the White House, his base of supplies. The Federal lines were now drawn close in front of the Chickahominy river and Grant now determined to attempt the passage of that River. There was a serious obstacle in the way, Lee's Army, & he massed his troops at & around Coal Harbor, with a view of making one more desperate effort to break through Lee's line, cross the Chickahominy, & push on to Richmond.

June 3d. On this day the second battle of Coal Harbor was fought. Fourteen successive assaults were made upon the Confederate lines, the Yankees fighting with unusual spirit & pertinacity; but they were driven back with great slaughter at every point, except one. Breckenridge's Division held one of those unfortunate salient angles in our works, and after repeated attacks by the enemy, was obliged to yield to overwhelming numbers and retire from the works. The Yankee success was, however, short lived, for Finnegan [Joseph Finegan] coming up with his Florida Brigade and the Maryland Battalion, drove the enemy from the captured works and reestablished our line at that point. In vain did the Yankees strive to drive Finnegan out until, convinced by his sturdy resistance of the impossibility of accomplishing anything in that direction, they fell back to

---

Grant's right flank and pushed back a large body of skirmishers but did not rout the entire flank as Seymour suggests. Further proof of Seymour's dating error is that records show that Colonel Lester, whom he mentions next, was killed on June 2, not June 1. Foote, *Civil War*, III, 287; Booth, comp., *Records of Louisiana Confederate Soldiers*, Vol. III, Book I, 738.

43. DeBlanc suffered a great deal in the war. Captured at the second Battle of Fredericksburg, he was exchanged in time to fight at Gettysburg and be wounded there. Sadly, he was wounded again the day after taking command of the brigade and was forced to retire in August, 1864. Booth, comp., *Records of Louisiana Confederate Soldiers*, II, 572–73.

their works and abandoned the Chickahominy route to the Confederate Capital. This second battle of Coal harbor resulted, as did the first one, in a glorious victory to the Confederate arms. Federal authorities estimated Grant's loss at six thousand men, though there were palpable evidences of a much greater loss. The Confederate loss did not exceed one thousand.[44]

Grant having been forced to the conviction that Richmond could not be taken from the North side of the James River determined to transfer his army to the South of that stream & connect his lines with those of Butler's Army. Butler had signally failed in his attempt upon Petersburg, and in turn had been driven by Beauregard a considerable distance down the James to Bermuda Hundred.[45]

June 4th. Intelligence having been received that the Federal General [David] Hunter with an army of twenty thousand men was advancing up the Valley of the Shenandoah towards Staunton, with a view of proceeding to Lynchburg & by the capture of that place put into execution one of the original plans of the Campaign; Sigel's attempt to do the same having, as I have already mentioned, met with a signal & disastrous failure. Our Corps & Breckenridge's Division were put in motion on this day, the 4th, to arrest Hunter's advance. Breckenridge's Division went by rail to Charlottesville, while Early's Corps took up the line of march for Lynchburg.[46] On the 5th inst. Hunter met & defeated a vastly inferior Cavalry force under Gen. W[illiam] E. Jones at Piedmont & in consequence, Staunton fell into his hands. In this engagement Gen. Jones was killed; he was one of the bravest, most skillful & active Cavalry commanders in the Confederate service, and his death was universally lamented.

44. The tragic June 3 assault at Cold Harbor would haunt Grant forever. Being impatient, he failed to reconnoiter or plan the assault well and sent his men into a wall of flaming muskets. In less than thirty minutes he lost approximately seven thousand men while Lee suffered only fifteen hundred casualties. Foote, *Civil War,* III, 289–92.

45. As part of Grant's great 1864 offensive, Butler was to take nearly forty thousand men and attack Richmond by way of the James River. Lacking aggressiveness and talent, Butler was "bottled up" by Beauregard on Bermuda Hundred, a peninsula formed by the James River. To break the stalemate with Lee, Grant planned to disengage and swing wide to the south, bypassing Richmond, to attack Petersburg. There he could use Bermuda Hundred as a base and cut the supply lines to Lee and Richmond. *Ibid.,* 312–17; Faust, *Encyclopedia of the Civil War,* 57–58.

46. For some reason, Seymour errs on the date Early left for the Valley. Lee did not receive word of Hunter's presence until June 5. To meet this threat he dispatched Breckinridge to Lynchburg on June 7. Then, upon learning that Hunter had captured Lexington, Lee finally sent Early's corps to aid Breckinridge on June 13. Freeman, *R. E. Lee,* III, 392–402.

Breckenridge posted his troops in such a manner as to guard the pass through the mountains lying between Staunton & Charlottesville, and Hunter was obliged to take the road to Lynchburg via Lexington. A race now began between Breckenridge & Hunter as to which should get to Lynchburg first. Hunter had by far the best road, but his progress was so much impeded by Gen. [John] McCausland's Cavalry Brigade, who blocked up the roads at every available point & skirmished constantly with the enemy's advance, that Breckenridge was obliged to win the race & reach Lynchburg a few hours in advance of his antagonist. On discovering this, Hunter crossed the James [River] a few miles above Lynchburg, intending to take that city from the South. But he found the wary Breckenridge again in the front. On the 18th inst. an attack was made upon Breckenridge's works, which was handsomely repulsed. On the next day, while Hunter was disposing his troops for another & more general attack, Early came up & greatly disconcerted the plans of the Federal commander. That night Early made preparations for an assault the next day upon the Yankees which, if it had been carried into execution, would inevitably had resulted in the discomfiture and capture of Hunter's Army. But at day light next morning, it was discovered that Hunter had fled in confusion in a South Westerly direction; Early rapidly pursued him as far as Salem, capturing thirteen pieces of artillery & a large portion of his Commissary & Quartermaster stores & forcing him to a line of retreat into the mountains of Western Virginia.

On the 4th of June I was ordered by the Brigade Surgeon to [the] Hospital in Richmond, I being too sick to continue at my post. For a month previous to the opening of the Campaign on the 4th of May, I had been very unwell & was advised by the Chief Surgeon of the Brigade to go to the rear; but I did not like the idea of leaving my post at the threshold of the campaign, so I remained on duty until after the battle of Coal Harbor, when my disease becoming more aggravated, I was forced to give up & go to [the] Hospital on the 10th of June. After remaining at the Louisiana Hospital for four days, I was ordered to appear before the Board of Examing [sic] Surgeons, who gave me a leave of absence of fifty days, which was afterwards extended twenty days. This time I spent with my Wife and child at Augusta, Georgia.

THE CAMPAIGN OF GENERAL
EARLY IN THE VALLEY

I T is not known what illness Seymour contracted in the spring of 1864, but his sick furlough is included in the Seymour Papers. Evidence indicates that he must have been absent from the brigade from June 10 until the end of August. During that time Early chased Hunter from the Valley and caused havoc in Maryland. Lee's orders stipulated that Early move down the Valley into Maryland after Hunter's force was dispersed. It was hoped that, besides collecting supplies, he could threaten Washington and Baltimore, forcing Grant to strip his army to reinforce those cities.[1]

On the afternoon of July 9, Early was forced to do battle with General Lew Wallace at the Monocacy River, Maryland. Gordon's division made a determined assault on the federal left that broke through three lines of defense and ultimately sent the Yankees flying. Brigadier General Zebulon York, commanding the Louisiana Brigade, claimed it was one of the bloodiest and fiercest battles of his life considering the numbers engaged. He wrote that the brigade lost one-fourth of its men, but precise casualties were not reported. The entire division lost 698 men. Wallace suffered almost 2,000 casualties.[2] Seymour missed out on this action but rejoined the brigade in time to participate in the bloody Valley Campaign that followed.

G EN. Early, after reaching Salem, withdrew from the pursuit of Hunter in that direction and directed his march to Staunton & thence down the Valley of the Shenandoah. In July he crossed the Potomac into Maryland & took up his line of march for Washington. At the Bridge across the

---

1. Lee's orders to Early were to eliminate the threat from Hunter's force and then move down the Valley into Maryland. *OR*, Vol. XXXVII, Pt. I, 346.
2. *Ibid.*, 350–52; Frank E. Vandiver, *Jubal's Raid: General Early's Famous Attack on Wash-*

Monocacy River—near Frederick City—our Division (Gordon's) met & after a stubborn fight against four times our own number, whipped the Yankee Corps under Gen. [Lew] Wallace. This was one of the sharpest & most bloody fights of the war and our Brigade lost fully one half of the men that went into action, including several of our best officers.

Upon arriving in front of Washington, Early found that Grant had reinforced the place heavily from his Army of the Potomac, making the force there too strong for him to attack with any chances of a successful issue; so he marched back to the Shenandoah Valley & there waited the pursuit of the Yankees. This movement against Washington, though unsuccessful as far as the capture of the city was contemplated, had the desired effect of drawing away from Grant one whole Corps (the 6th) and two Divisions of another, thereby greatly relieving Gen. Lee of the pressure upon his lines around Richmond & Petersburg.

An expedition had been fitted out at Wilmington, N[orth] C[arolina], for the purpose of co-operating with Early; this expedition consisted of two swift running "blockaders," having on board two full batteries of field artillery, twelve hundred troops, and seven thousand muskets. It was under the command of Gen. Custis Lee (son of Gen. Robt. E. Lee) and was intended to capture Point Lookout, on the East Maryland shore of the Chesapeake Bay, release the eleven thousand Confederate prisoners incarcerated there, arm them & march upon Washington from the South while Early approached it from the North West. Had the steamer succeeded in getting out of Wilmington, there is but little doubt that Point Lookout could have been taken. But unfortunately the requisite secrecy was not observed in the fitting out of the expedition, and consequently the commander of the Federal Blockading Squadron was informed of its time of sailing, destination, etc., so that when the two ships attempted to run out under cover of the darkness of the night, Lee found, to his great astonishment & chagrin, that every outlet from the harbor was so strongly & effectually guarded by the Yankee

ington in 1864 (New York, 1960), 110–18; Zebulon York to B. B. Wellford, July 18, 1864, in White, Wellford, Taliaferro, and Marshall Collection, Southern Historical Collection, University of North Carolina, Chapel Hill.

steamers that escape was impossible, and he was forced to return to Wilmington & abandon the enterprise.[3]

Gen. Early having fallen back to the Opequon River, in the Valley of the Shenandoah, was soon followed by Hunter with a largely superior force & compelled to retreat to Fisher's Hill, where he made a stand. Hunter declined to attack him and retreated down the Valley to Harper's Ferry, eagerly pressured by Early. For several weeks Gen. Early, by a series of bold, masterly maneuvers, kept the Yankee Army at bay, though it was at least four times larger than his own.[4]

In September [Philip] Sheridan assumed the command of the Federal Army & advanced against Early who was lying behind the Opequon, six miles from Winchester. Finding that Sheridan had massed nearly his whole force near Berryville, Gen. Early sent our Division (Gordon's) to Martinsburg, where we arrived on the 18th of September. There we found only a couple of cavalry Brigades of the enemy, which a portion of our Brigade, assisted by a section of artillery, attacked & routed. After tearing down two miles of telegraph wire we returned to Bunker Hill that night—twelve miles distant from Winchester.

At day-break next morning, we resumed our march. At 8 A.M. as we reached our old position, we heard the distant booming of cannon that told but too plainly that the enemy had commenced the attack upon [Gabriel Colvin] Wharton's & Ramseur's Divisions, which guarded the South bank of the Opequon.[5] Sheridan threw his whole force against those small Divisions, which after a most stubborn & gallant resistance, were driven back, fighting as they went, to within two miles of Winchester. The arrival of our Division on the field at 10 o'clock was most opportune and stopped the further progress of the enemy towards Winchester. Forming on the left of Ramseur, we had barely deployed into line when the Yankees were

3. Early went so far as to send Brigadier General Bradley Johnson's cavalry brigade toward Point Lookout to cooperate with the amphibious attack, but the brigade returned when the attempt was abandoned. Foote, *Civil War*, III, 449, 459.

4. Early had about 8,500 men at the beginning of September, 1864, and the Yankees mustered approximately 35,000. *OR*, Vol. XLIII, Pt. I, 1002–1003; Faust, *Encyclopedia of the Civil War*, 835.

5. When Sheridan received intelligence that part of Early's army had been sent to Martinsburg, he decided to hit Early's weakened force on the Opequon. *OR*, Vol. XLIII, Pt. I, 46–47.

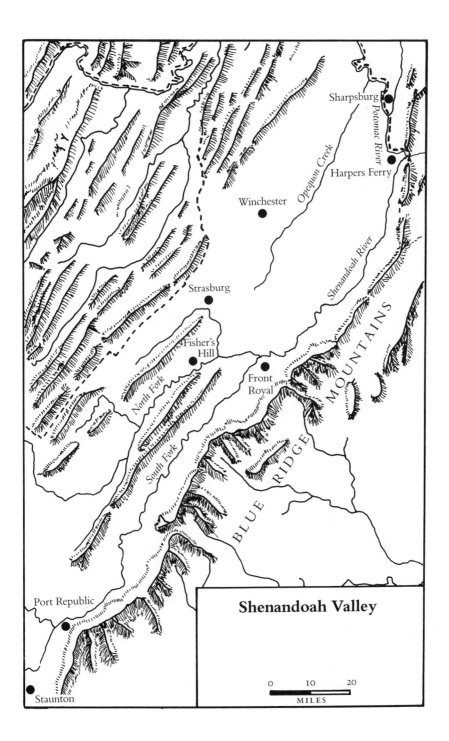

Sharpsburg

Potomac River

Harpers Ferry

Opequon Creek

Winchester

Shenandoah River

Strasburg

Fisher's Hill

North Fork

Front Royal

South Fork

B L U E   R I D G E   M O U N T A I N S

Port Republic

Staunton

Shenandoah Valley

0   10   20

MILES

seen advancing at a charge against us; our Brigade was ordered by Gen. Early to advance, and the beautiful & rare sight was presented of two opposing lines charging at the same time. Though the Yankees fought unusually well, they could not withstand the impetuosity of our fellows and they were forced back upon their original line which was strongly guarded by artillery.[6]

We had reformed & were about to make a dash upon this line, when the two Brigades on our left ([Clement] Evans' & Terry's) which had charged with us, but which we got far in advance of, unaccountably gave way, leaving us in a very perilous situation, and we were obliged to fall back about one hundred yds. to prevent our flank from being turned. The cause of the above mentioned break in our line was said to be the neglect of the commander of the 60th Georgia Regt., which held the extreme left of the line, to order his men to load their guns, he alleging as a reason that he had not received the necessary orders from his superior officer. Then this regiment, advancing through a piece of woods, came suddenly upon the Yankee line charging at the same time; the men with their muskets unloaded could not stand before the withering fire that was poured upon them and they fled in confusion, followed in a few minutes by the other Regts. of the Brigade & by Terry's Virginia Brigade.[7]

This *contretemps* came near losing us the battle at that early hour of the day, for if the enemy had followed up their success and effected a permanent lodgement between the two wings of our Army, the left wing would have been entirely cut off from communication with Winchester, & consequently from all chance of retreat up the Valley upon our base of supplies. But just at this critical moment, Rodes' splendid Division came upon the ground at a double-quick, & quickly forming line of battle, charged forward with the greatest elan, driving the "blue coats" back to their old position and restor-

---

6. The toe-to-toe fight with the Yankees must have been impressive. G. P. Ring wrote his wife that it was "the prettiest stand up fair open fight that I have ever seen." The two lines traded volleys at two hundred yards for ten minutes before the Yankees fell back. The Louisianians chased after them and "poured a fire into their backs that soon made the ground black with their hateful bodies." Ring claimed that the brigade fought its best fight of the war at the Opequon and attributed its performance to rumors that a federal Louisiana regiment was opposing it. G. P. Ring to wife, September 21, 1864, in Army of Northern Virginia Papers, Part I.

7. Ring identified the regiment that first broke as the 61st Georgia. *Ibid.*

ing our own line. While this movement was in progress, a bullet pierced the brain of the gallant Gen. Rodes & he fell from his horse about ten paces from where I was standing. Thus died one of the best Division Commanders in the Army of Northern Virginia—an intrepid & accomplished soldier, and a gentleman of many noble qualities & of unaffected & attractive manners. On account of the remarkable skill & bravery he displayed on the battle field of Chancellorsville, Gen. "Stonewall" Jackson, while on his death bed, recommended his promotion; on the following day he recd. his commission as Major General.[8]

For four hours & a half our little army of *eight thousand five hundred* muskets repulsed charge after charge of the Federal infantry, *thirty-five thousand strong*. It was one of the hardest fought battles of the war and we would have gained the victory had our cavalry been strong enough to cope with the large & well appointed cavalry force of Sheridan. Gen. Early's cavalry force amounted to about *three thousand men,* mostly armed with long Enfield rifles, & for the most part without sabres or pistols, while Sheridan had *ten thousand one hundred men,* (as shown by official statements captured subsequently at Cedar Creek) splendidly armed and equipped.

About 4½ o'clock P.M., Sheridan massed all of his cavalry on our left, advanced up the Martinsburg turnpike & driving easily before him our small & badly armed cavalry force, attained our rear & charged us in flank & rear. One of Wharton's Brigades of infantry, under Col. Forberg [Augustus Forsberg], on the extreme left, was severely handled, a great many of the men being sabred. Our situation at this time was extremely critical; in front of us was the enemy's infantry four times larger than our own, while in the rear on the flank of our left wing was his cavalry which of itself outnumbered our infantry. Of course, there was nothing left but to retreat and as soon as the order was given, our line broke & the men poured through Winchester in the greatest confusion. Early's artillery (40 pieces) fought to the last, many of the guns remaining on the ground unsupported by infantry until their amunition chests were entirely emptied. The admirable manner in which the Artillerists served their guns prevented Sheridan from rapidly pursuing our demor-

8. One historian claims that the only officer Jackson praised while on his deathbed was a Colonel Edward Willis. Dowdey, *Lee's Last Campaign*, 280.

alized troops & enabled our train to escape. That night our army was in rapid flight up the Valley.

The battle of Winchester, or Opequon, was lost by Gen. Early through no fault of his or of his troops; but he was overpowered by the superior numbers of the enemy. Some of his Cavalry behaved badly, but this is not to be wondered at when we take into consideration their weakness in numbers and the inferior quality of their arms.

To illustrate the ardent patriotism of the ladies of Winchester, I will here state the remarkable fact that when a number of [John Daniel] Imboden's Cavalry rushed pell mell through the streets of that city, far in advance of all other fugitives from the battle field, a large number of the most respected ladies joined hands & formed a line across the principal street, telling the cowardly Cavalrymen that they should not go any further unless they ran their horses over their bodies. In this manner a large number of demoralized & fugacious cavalrymen were induced to return to the fight. Mrs. Gordon, wife of the General Commanding our Division, who accompanied her husband through all the arduous marches and perilous scenes of the Valley Campaign, seized the bridle of a recreant Cavalryman & leading his horse down Main St. to the edge of the town, told him to return to the battle-field or dismount & surrender to her his horse & gun, that she might take his place. It is needless to say that the man returned to his post of duty.[9]

The Federals took five pieces of artillery from Gen. Early—all of them captured from our cavalry. Our Brigade (Hays' & Stafford's) lost several good officers. Gen. [Zebulon] York, Comdg., was shot in the wrist & had his arm amputated;[10] Cols. Peck & [Eugene] Waggoman [Waggaman], the first Comdg. Hays' & the last Stafford's Brigades, were wounded, but not seriously.[11] So hot was the

9. Mrs. Gordon was a busy woman. Ring claimed that she grabbed the divisional headquarters flag, called for the division to rally, and led two hundred men back to the front. Ring to wife, September 21, 1864, in Army of Northern Virginia Papers, Part I.

10. York, former colonel of the 14th Louisiana, won his brigadier star and brigade command in June, 1864—the only Confederate of Polish descent to do so. He was known for his bravery and for being one of the army's most voracious swearers. Jones, *Lee's Tigers,* 208; Warner, *Generals in Gray,* 347–48; Sigmund H. Uminski, "Poles and the Confederacy," *Polish American Studies,* XXII (1965), 102.

11. Peck later replaced the wounded York as brigade commander and was promoted to brigadier general in early 1865. Colonel Waggaman of the 10th Louisiana helped cover the

fire, that of eight officers who went into the fight mounted, seven had their horses either killed or wounded. My horse was shot in the knee & I had to abandon him.[12]

That night (the 19th) we continued the retreat up the Valley until 12 o'clock, when we halted and bivoucked until morning. At dawn of day on the 20th, we resumed the march and reached Fisher's Hill at 10 o'clock & formed line of battle behind the old breastworks that Early had constructed six weeks previously, when pursued by Hunter. Our force was greatly reduced at this time, for a large number of the men had fled to the mountains, but these came in the next day. Surgeon [William S.] Love, who had been left in Winchester to take charge of the wounded of our army, reported to me that they numbered 430; while those of the enemy amounted to twenty-six hundred. Our whole loss in the battle of Winchester was estimated at 1,200 men.[13]

On the morning of the 21st of September great clouds of dust appeared hanging over the Martinsburg pike, indicating the advance of the enemy. The position of our Brigade lay on the top of a high hill, the approach of the enemy could be distinctly seen with the aid of a glass and an animating spectacle it was. First came about five thousand cavalry, their arms glistening in the sun; then long columns of infantry, followed by immense trains of ambulances & waggons; & after them came the artillery. As they came within two miles of our line, they filed off to the right & left & the remainder of the day was occupied by the Yankees in taking position preparatory to an assault upon our works. Towards night the enemy felt of our line in several places by advancing his skirmish line; in front of the position of our Brigade our sharpshooters, deployed as skirmishers, repelled three attacks of the Yankees in line of battle. No general attack was made during this day.

The morning of the 22d was passed by the enemy in maneuvring

---

retreat despite his wound. He was seen riding into the melee, fighting wildly, with his horse's reins held between his teeth. Warner, *Generals in Gray*, 231; Bartlett, *Military Record of Louisiana*, 37.

12. The only known casualty list for the Louisiana Brigade is found in the above-mentioned Ring letter. Ring placed the brigade's losses at 154. Ring to wife, September 21, 1864, in Army of Northern Virginia Papers, Part I.

13. Early put his losses at 226 dead, 1,567 wounded, and 1,818 missing. Sheridan lost a little over 5,000 men. *OR*, Vol. XLIII, Pt. I, 556; Faust, *Encyclopedia of the Civil War*, 835.

& skirmishing, with an occasional interchange of shots between the hostile batteries. About 1 o'clock P.M. I was ordered to select an officer to relieve the one in command of the sharpshooters. I selected Capt. Weightman, of the 9th Regt., who had returned to the Brigade on that day, having been to the rear on account of a wound in the head recd. in one of our encounters in July with Sheridan's Cavalry. At my solicitation, he exchanged his officer's uniform for the coat of a private in order that he might be a less conspicuous mark for the enemy's sharpshooters. Poor fellow, he had not been ten minutes on the line before he recd. a mortal wound. When he fell, several of his men made their way to him under a shower of bullets, for the purpose of conveying him to the rear; but he ordered them to their posts, saying that since Fate had decreed that he should fall, he wished to die on the skirmish line, in the midst of the noble fellows that composed his corps of sharpshooters. He breathed his last a few minutes afterwards. Capt. Weightman was a tall, handsome, young man of 22 yrs. of age—of many excellent qualities of head & heart & as a soldier possessed of rare coolness & bravery in action.[14]

The Yankees advanced against our extreme right & the centre but it was easily seen that their attack upon those points were only feints; and we soon saw that their design was to turn our left flank. The force of infantry that Gen. Early had under his command was inadequate to fill out the whole line of works, so he dismounted [William Lowther] Jackson's & Imboden's Brigades of cavalry & placed them on the extreme left of the line. It was against this portion of our works, thus poorly defended, that the enemy directed his attack. Sheridan sent a force up the side of the mountain, thereby turning our left, while at the same time several lines of battle bore down upon our dismounted Cavalry. Jackson's men broke & fled & the enemy swept down our line from left to right with irrisistible force. Our Division remained in the works until nearly surrounded, when the order being given to retreat, we stood not on the order of our going; it was altogether too late to retire in order, for it required the greatest fleetness of foot to enable us to keep from being captured. We fell back up the Turnpike towards New Market; the en-

14. Strangely, there is no record of a Captain Weightman serving in any of the brigade's regiments.

emy, being satisfied with the capture of our works, did not pressure us vigorously that night. A section of artillery under direction of Col. [Alexander S.] Pendleton did a great deal towards retarding pursuit. The Col. was killed, he was the A[ssistant] A[djutant] Genl. of Gen. Early & had served with distinction in the same capacity on the Staff of the lamented Stonewall Jackson. His loss was universally lamented.[15]

We marched until 2 o'clock in the morning when we halted until daylight, when we resumed our retreat to New Market. Here we formed line of battle & awaited the arrival of the enemy. The Yankees coming up in the afternoon, we fell back in line & in excellent order, the enemy's batteries played upon us in the most lively manner, while the sharpshooters of the two armies kept up a rattling fusilade. This continued until we reached the vicinity of Harrisonburg, when we left the Valley pike & struck across the country in the direction of Brown's Gap—a place that had been on several occasions resorted to by Gen. Jackson when hard pressed by the superior forces of the enemy. The Corps' Ordnance train was sent across the mountains (the Blue Ridge) but the troops remained between the South Fork of the Shenandoah & the Gap. Sheridan's infantry stopped at Harrisonburg and his cavalry followed us, at a respectful distance, as far as Port Republic on the opposite side of the river, but made no attempt to cross.

On the evening of the 24th & the morning of the 25th of September, there was considerable skirmishing between the hostile forces, but the enemy's cavalry dared not come to close quarter with our infantry, though they outnumbered us. On the 26th, our Division (Gordon's) & that of Pegram, crossed the river some four miles South of Port Republic for the purpose of getting on the flank of the enemy and taking them by surprise—Ramseur's and Wharton's Divisions being ordered to attack them in front as soon as we opened fire. The crossing was quietly and successfully effected, and our troops marched up the road leading to the somewhat famous Weir's [Weyers] Cave.[16] This Cave is one five miles in length and is divided

15. Early suffered a loss of 30 dead, 210 wounded, and a staggering 995 missing at the Fisher's Hill debacle. *OR*, Vol. XLIII, Pt. I, 556.

16. Weyers Cave is located near Grottoes, Virginia, and is now a famous tourist attraction called Grand Caverns.

into rooms, some of which are said to be remarkably regular in their formation. It so happened that when we crossed the river, there were a large number of Yankee officers in this Cave on a tour of exploration, some of them being Generals of high rank. These wonder-seeking gentlemen of the shoulder-strap would have been surprised and captured had it not been for the indiscreetness of an artillery officer who commanded a section of guns that accompanied our advance guard. On arriving at an elevated point within a few hundred yards of the Cave, this officer espied a large force of the enemy's cavalry massed in a plain within easy range of his guns; the temptation was too strong, so, without awaiting order, he blazed away away [sic] at the unsuspecting Yankees, producing the greatest & most ludicrous disorder in their ranks. This premature opening of the fight acted as a warning to the officers in the Cave, who speedily terminated their exploration, mounted their horses and fled in safety to the main body. It is needless to say that this impudent discharge of artillery brought forth, in return, a tremendous volley of oaths from the irascible and emphatic Gen. Early upon the offending officer.

Our force was quickly formed in line of battle; our Brigade, deployed as skirmishers, occupying the extreme left when we advanced under quite a spirited fire of artillery and musketry. The enemy, fearing to be caught in the elbow formed by the two forks of the Shenandoah, fell back before our troops, crossed the North Fork, and retired in the direction of Harrisonburg, Sheridan's Head Quarters; our artillery considerably accelerated the speed of the retreating blue-coats. The enemy's troopers were too fleet for our "foot cavalry," and but very few prisoners were taken by us. In company with Genl. Pegram and Major New, I crossed the North Fork and went on a short scouting excursion as far as the battle field of Cross Keys.[17] All the Yankees had gone but one cavalryman belonging to a Pennsylvania Regt., who was so terribly wounded by a shell from one of our guns that he could not be moved. The General spoke to him kindly, promised to send an ambulance for him, & I gave him a couple of opium pills.

On the next day, the 27th, the army took up it's line of march to

17. On June 8, 1862, near the end of his famous Valley Campaign, Stonewall Jackson defeated General John C. Frémont at Cross Keys. Faust, *Encyclopedia of the Civil War*, 195.

Waynesboro, a small town ten miles east of Staunton; this move was caused by a raid which was in progress against those places and the Railroad leading to Lynchburg, consisting of a Division of Federal Cavalry under Gen. [Alfred T. A. Torbert] Torbett. The Yankees succeeded in destroying the public stores at Staunton, and tearing up the Railroad between that place and Waynesboro. When our advance guard, under Genl. Pegram, arrived at Waynesboro, they found the enemy making an attempt to reach & destroy the long tunnel near that place; but they were successfully held at bay by a gallant party of citizens—some of them mere boys—who defended the place most nobly. Gen. Pegram, after a little brisk skirmishing, put Torbett's raiders to flight.[18] Our Division, which brought up the rear of the army, did not reach the vicinity of Waynesboro until late at night, when we went into camp after a most fatiguing march.

Here we remained until the morning of the 30th of September, when we marched down the Valley again, crossing from the Waynesboro road to the Valley pike, striking it at a place called "The Willow Pump." This little settlement takes it's name from the fact that on the side of the pike at that point, a steady & abundant stream of pure, cool water gushes forth from a hole in the trunk of a Willow tree, coming up from a spring concealed from view under the roots of the tree.

We proceeded some two miles beyond Mt. Jackson, where we went into camp; here we remained until the 7th of October. Early, finding that Sheridan had abandoned his position at Harrisonburg and gone down the Valley to Strasburg, moved his army on the 6th inst. to New Market, & a few days afterward to Fisher's Hill, thus affording Sheridan an opportunity to attack him again at that point. Early had been reinforced by Kershaw's small Division, 2,400 strong, and burned to have another trial of strength & valor with the Yankees at Fisher's Hill; but Sheridan contented himself with lying behind his fortifications.

Information having been received that Sheridan had left with one Corps, the 6th, Gen. Early resolved to attack the two Corps which

18. Sheridan sent Torbert up the Luray Valley to New Market in an attempt to cut off Early's retreat, but the Yankees failed after encountering Fitz Lee's cavalry. Torbert then tried to destroy the railroad tunnel at Rockfish Gap. There he was again foiled by a company of young reservists and two cannons. These reservists must have been the "civilians" Seymour is referring to. Early, *War Memoirs*, 434–35; Foote, *Civil War*, III, 557.

remained in his front though either of them was larger than his whole army.[19] On the night of the 18th the requisite preparations were made to surprise the enemy's camp at dawn on the following day; Gordon's & Pegram's (Rodes') Divisions were selected to attack the enemy's left flank, while Kershaw's, Ramseur's & Wharton's were to attack their front. A little after dark the first named Divisions were put in light marching order, the men being divested of their canteens & everything that could rattle or make a noise so that they could get as near as possible to the enemy before the movement should be detected. Gen. Gordon, who commanded this portion of the expedition, led his men far around to the right of the enemy & for a considerable distance over a mountain path which was so narrow that the men had to march in single file. So quietly and skillfully was the march conducted, that, notwithstanding the two divisions had to pass for almost the whole distance within a very short distance of the Yankee picket lines, it was nearly day break before our advance guard came in collision with the enemy's videttes. At the crossing of Cedar Creek, Gordon was fired upon by a small picket force of cavalry, who fled precipitately at his approach. He pushed on with the greatest celerity in the direction of Belle Grove, where was the Yankee camps & entrenchments. Arriving there before the alarm had been given he charged upon the astonished Yankees with the greatest impetuosity; at the same moment the other Divisions attacked in front, capturing a large fort that commanded the road to Winchester.

19. Sheridan had started the VI Corps on its way to reinforce Grant, but it would return and participate in the coming battle at Cedar Creek. Foote, *Civil War*, III, 564.

EPILOGUE

SEYMOUR'S narrative abruptly ends midway through the Battle of Cedar Creek. In that fight the Confederates swept through and captured the federal camps. But instead of pursuing the defeated Yankees, the rebels stopped to plunder. This gave Sheridan time to regroup his shaken command and mount a counterattack that crushed Early's force. This decisive Union victory was the last major engagement in the Valley.[1] In December, 1864, the remnants of the Louisiana Brigade were sent to Petersburg, Virginia, to join Lee's beleaguered army. The survivors surrendered with Lee at Appomattox on April 9, 1865.

Why the narrative ended so suddenly is unknown. Perhaps Seymour wrote his memoirs late in life and illness forced him to stop, or the narrative might have been continued in another volume that has been lost. It does not seem likely that Seymour would have stopped writing in midstory. The narrative is long and detailed, and two versions were written, indicating that much time was put into the project. Also, Seymour's journalistic background would seem to preclude his willingly leaving a story unfinished.

Without his detailed writings, it is very difficult to follow Seymour through the rest of the war. In early October, 1864, he fell ill with fever and diarrhea and received extended sick leave. His military record shows that he was absent sick from the brigade from October 10, 1864, until at least February 27, 1865. During part of that time he was admitted to the Ladies Relief Hospital and a general hospital, both in Lynchburg, Virginia.[2]

---

1. *OR*, Vol. XXXXIII, Pt. I, 561–64; Faust, *Encyclopedia of the Civil War*, 121.
2. Compiled Service Records of Confederate General and Staff Officers, War Record Group 109, Microcopy 331, Roll 223, National Archives; undated surgeon's transfer order, in Seymour Papers.

On January 16, 1865, Seymour requested a transfer to Louisiana or someplace else in the "extreme south," citing his failing health as a reason. But apparently brigade politics and personal ambition also played a role in his decision. On January 21, 1864, Seymour had written Lieutenant General Leonidas Polk in Georgia, requesting an appointment to his staff. Seymour reminded Polk that the general had offered such a position at about the same time Seymour had joined Hays's staff. Now in 1864, Seymour noted that it appeared Hays would be promoted to a divisional command. In that case, another officer (presumably Peck or Monaghan) would take over the 1st Louisiana Brigade. Without elaborating, Seymour told Polk that if this happened, "I will not be as pleasantly situated with the [new] officer" as he was with Hays. Besides this unstated personal conflict, Seymour unabashedly told Polk, "I am very anxious to obtain an increase of rank."[3] Seymour was not appointed to Polk's staff, but later, while ill in early 1865, he again requested a transfer. Although he cited health concerns as his reasons, it must be assumed that his desire for a promotion and the personal conflict he mentioned earlier were still contributing factors. There is no official record showing that Seymour got his transfer southward, although he did request on February 11, 1865, to be allowed to travel to Macon, Georgia, and join his family while awaiting orders.[4]

Apparently Seymour did receive a transfer. Postwar newspaper articles state that late in the war he was appointed inspector general on the staff of Major General Pierce Manning Butler Young. Young, a Georgian, was one of Lee's cavalry brigadiers dispatched to Augusta, Georgia, in November, 1864, to defend that city against William T. Sherman's approaching army. Seymour also may have received his long-awaited promotion. Postwar articles also refer to him as "Major" Seymour (one placing him in the artillery), although again there is no confirming record. General Young's command continued to fight Sherman's army as it marched through the Carolinas in early 1865, but it is not known whether Seymour participated in the campaign.[5]

3. Compiled Service Records of Confederate General and Staff Officers, War Record Group 109, Microcopy 331, Roll 223, National Archives.
4. *Ibid.*
5. *Ibid.*, Roll 275; Seymour obituary, November 15, 1886, newspaper clipping, in Sey-

When the war was over, Seymour took his family back to New Orleans, eventually settling in a house on Pelus Street, where he apparently wrote his narrative. He immediately plunged back into the publishing business, becoming an editor for the *Daily Democrat,* as well as being associated with the *Commercial Bulletin* and another local paper. In 1868, Seymour fulfilled an outstanding obligation to his deceased father. When traveling through Macon with his regiment in 1861, Colonel Seymour had told friends that if he were killed he would like to be buried in Macon beside his wife and children. In January, 1868, William returned to Lynchburg, Virginia, exhumed his father's body, and dutifully reinterred it in Macon's Rosewood Cemetery.[6]

Despite failing health caused by heart disease, Seymour remained active during the postwar years. He became adjutant of the 1st Louisiana Regiment (militia) and earned the title of colonel. Sometime during this period he also began writing his war memoirs, part of which he published in a local newspaper. Seymour began his narrative with the bombardment of Fort Jackson, claiming that his purpose was to correct misrepresentations made by Union reports on the siege. Some passages of his Fort Jackson narrative were almost verbatim from General Duncan's official report. There are two possible explanations for this. Since Duncan's report was released as part of the voluminous *The War of the Rebellion: A Compilation of the Official Records of the Union and Confederate Armies* a few years before Seymour's death, he could have taken the liberty of using it. Or, because Seymour was Duncan's aide during the bombardment and kept a diary during the siege, Seymour might have helped Duncan draw up his report, using the diary as a guide. This would explain the similarities in the two, since Seymour also used his diary as the basis for his memoirs. There are no other instances in the narrative suggesting Seymour might have copied the *Official Records,* so it would seem unlikely that he did so with the Fort Jackson material. Also, because people in New Orleans would have been familiar with Duncan's report in the *Official Records,* so prominent a jour-

---

mour Papers; undated newspaper clipping, *ibid.;* Warner, *Generals in Gray,* 348; Young, Gholson, and Hargrove, *History of Macon,* 308.

6. Young, Gholson, and Hargrove, *History of Macon,* 308; undated newspaper clipping, in Seymour Papers; Seymour obituary, November 15, 1886, newspaper clipping, *ibid.*

nalist as Seymour would not have taken a chance of being labeled a plagiarizer.[7]

During these postwar years Seymour was blessed with children, which by 1886 numbered five, three others having died in infancy. Perhaps to accommodate his growing brood, Seymour moved his family to a house at 195 Thalia Street. But he did not live to see all his children grow up. His failing heart forced him to retire from his newspapers, and he even moved temporarily to the North in an attempt to nurse himself back to health. When this failed, he returned to New Orleans, where on November 14, 1886, he died quietly from chronic heart disease. Thus passed a witness to one of the epic chapters of our country's history. His service carried him to several theaters of war and left him with a perspective that came from the headquarters as well as the firing line. Not content to be swept along as a faceless participant, Seymour became a chronicler who left succeeding generations a colorful impression of the drudgery, horror, pomp, and glory of the Civil War.[8]

7. Seymour obituary, November 15, 1886, newspaper clipping, in Seymour Papers; Ex-officer, "Bombardment of Forts Jackson and St. Philip," *ibid.*
8. Seymour obituary, November 15, 1886, newspaper clipping, *ibid.*

BIBLIOGRAPHY

MANUSCRIPT SOURCES

Duke University, Durham, North Carolina
  Confederate Veteran Papers.
Library of Congress, Washington, D.C.
  Ewell, Richard S. Papers.
Louisiana State University, Baton Rouge
  Boyd, David F. Civil War Papers.
  Boyd, David F. Scrapbook.
  Egan, J. S. Family Papers.
National Archives, Washington, D.C.
  Compiled Service Records of Confederate General and Staff Officers, and
    Nonregimental Enlisted Men. War Record Group 109. Microcopy 331.
  Compiled Service Records of Confederate Soldiers Who Served in Organiza-
    tions from the State of Louisiana. War Record Group 109. Microcopy 320.
  Early, General Jubal A. Papers, 1861–65. War Record Group 109. Entry 118.
New York Public Library, Rare Books and Manuscripts Division, New York City
  Louisiana Troops. 7th Regiment Orderly Book, 1862–64.
Northwestern State University, Natchitoches, Louisiana
  Stephens, Judge Paul. Collection.
Tulane University, New Orleans
  Civil War Scrapbooks.
  Louisiana Collection. Biographical File.
  New Orleans Civil War Scrapbooks.
Tulane University, Louisiana Historical Association Collection, New Orleans
  Army of Northern Virginia. Papers.
  Association of the Army of Northern Virginia. Papers.
  Moore, Charles, Jr. Diary, 1861–65.
University of Michigan, Ann Arbor
  Seymour, Isaac G. Papers. Schoff Civil War Collection.
University of North Carolina, Southern Historical Collection, Chapel Hill
  Brown, Campbell. Collection.
  Hairston, Peter W. Collection.
  White, Wellford, Taliaferro, and Marshall Collection.
  Williams, Marguerite E. Collection.

FEDERAL GOVERNMENT PUBLICATIONS

The Official Atlas of the Civil War. New York, 1958.

Official Records of the Union and Confederate Navies in the War of the Rebellion. 30 vols. Washington, D.C., 1894–1922.

The War of the Rebellion: A Compilation of the Official Records of the Union and Confederate Armies. 130 vols. Washington, D.C., 1880–1901.

BOOKS

Bartlett, Napier. *Military Record of Louisiana.* Baton Rouge, 1964.

Booth, Andrew B., comp. *Records of Louisiana Confederate Soldiers and Louisiana Confederate Commands.* 3 vols. New Orleans, 1920.

Carter, Samuel, III. *Blaze of Glory: The Fight for New Orleans, 1814–1815.* New York, 1971.

Casey, Powell A. *Encyclopedia of Forts, Posts, Named Camps, and Other Military Installations in Louisiana, 1700–1981.* Baton Rouge, 1983.

Coddington, Edwin B. *The Gettysburg Campaign: A Study in Command.* New York, 1968.

Davis, Burke. *They Called Him Stonewall: A Life of Lt. General T. J. Jackson, C.S.A.* New York, 1954.

Dimitry, John. *Louisiana.* Atlanta, 1899. Vol. X of Clement Evans, ed., *Confederate Military History.* 10 vols.

Dowdey, Clifford. *Lee's Last Campaign: The Story of Lee and His Men Against Grant—1864.* Boston, 1960.

Early, Jubal Anderson. *A Memoir of the Last Year of the War for Independence . . . in the Year 1864 and 1865.* Lynchburg, 1867.

———. *War Memoirs: Autobiographical Sketch and Narrative of the War Between the States.* Edited by Frank E. Vandiver. 1912; rpr. Bloomington, 1960.

Espisito, Vincent J., ed. *The West Point Atlas of American Wars.* 2 vols. New York, 1959.

Evans, Clement A. *Georgia: Comprising Sketches of Counties, Towns, Events, Institutions and Persons. Arranged in Cyclopedic Form.* Edited by Allen D. Candler. 3 vols. Atlanta, 1906.

Faust, Patricia L., ed. *Historical Times Illustrated Encyclopedia of the Civil War.* New York, 1986.

Foote, Shelby. *The Civil War: A Narrative.* 3 vols. New York, 1958–74.

Freeman, Douglas Southall. *R. E. Lee: A Biography.* 4 vols. New York, 1935.

Jones, Terry L. *Lee's Tigers: The Louisiana Infantry in the Army of Northern Virginia.* Baton Rouge, 1987.

Kendall, John Smith. *History of New Orleans.* 3 vols. Chicago, 1922.

Klein, Margaret C. *Tombstone Inscriptions of Orange County, Virginia.* Baltimore, 1972.

Landry, Stuart. *History of the Boston Club.* New Orleans, 1938.

Malone, Dumas, ed. *Dictionary of American Biography.* 20 vols. New York, 1928–36.

Pratt, Fletcher. *Civil War on Western Waters*. New York, 1956.

Reed, Thomas Benton. *A Private in Gray*. Camden, Ark., 1905.

Robertson, James I., Jr. *General A. P. Hill: The Story of a Confederate Warrior*. New York, 1987.

Schurz, Carl. *The Reminiscences of Carl Schurz*. 3 vols. New York, 1907–1908.

Stackpole, Edward J. *Chancellorsville: Lee's Greatest Victory*. Harrisburg, 1958.

———. *Drama on the Rappahannock: The Fredericksburg Campaign*. Harrisburg, 1957.

Steere, Edward. *The Wilderness Campaign*. New York, 1960.

Thomas, Emory M. *Bold Dragoon: The Life of J. E. B. Stuart*. New York, 1986.

Vandiver, Frank E. *Jubal's Raid: General Early's Famous Attack on Washington in 1864*. New York, 1960.

Warner, Ezra J. *Generals in Blue: Lives of the Union Commanders*. Baton Rouge, 1964.

———. *Generals in Gray: Lives of the Confederate Commanders*. Baton Rouge, 1959.

Winters, John D. *The Civil War in Louisiana*. Baton Rouge, 1963.

Wise, Jennings Cropper. *The Long Arm of Lee: The History of the Artillery of the Army of Northern Virginia*. New York, 1959.

Yearns, Wilfred Buck. *The Confederate Congress*. Athens, Ga., 1960.

Young, Ida, Julius Gholson, and Clara Nell Hargrove. *History of Macon, Georgia*. Macon, 1950.

Journal Articles

Forman, William Harper, Jr. "William P. Harper in War and Reconstruction." *Louisiana History*, XIII (1972), 45–70.

Uminski, Sigmund H. "Poles and the Confederacy." *Polish American Studies*, XXII (1965), 99—106.

Newspapers

New Orleans *Times-Picayune*, December 26, 1915.

Interviews

Harrison, Doyle. August 5, 1987. Fredericksburg, Virginia.

Schley, Ben. November 5, 1987. Shepherdstown, West Virginia.

Waxham, Terry. October 28, 1987. Shreveport, Louisiana.

INDEX